CHORUS

'Cause I'm a jay, jay, jay, jay, jay-hawk up at Law-rence on the Kaw,_____ 'Cause I'm a jay, jay, jay, jay, jay-hawk, With a sis - boom hip hoo - rah,_____ Got a bill that's big e-nough to twist the tig-er's tail, Husk some corn and lis-ten to the corn-husk-er's wail 'Cause I'm a jay, jay, jay, jay, jay-hawk, Rid-ing on a 'Kan - sas gale._____ 'Cause I'm a gale, and that's our team._____

I'm A Jay Hawk 2

CRIMSON and BLUE

Far above the golden valley,
  Glorious to view,
Stands our noble Alma Mater
  Towering toward the blue.

CHORUS

Lift the chorus ever onward,
  Crimson and the Blue.
Hail to thee, our Alma Mater,
  Hail to K. S. U.

Far above the distant humming
  Of the busy town,
Reared against the dome of heaven,
  Looks she proudly down.

Greet we then our foster mother,
  Noble friend so true,
We will ever sing her praises,
  Dear old K. S. U.

THE STORY
OF
THE UNIVERSITY OF KANSAS

Monroe Dodd

THE UNIVERSITY OF KANSAS 1865–2015

KANSAS CITY STAR BOOKS

KANSAS CITY, MISSOURI

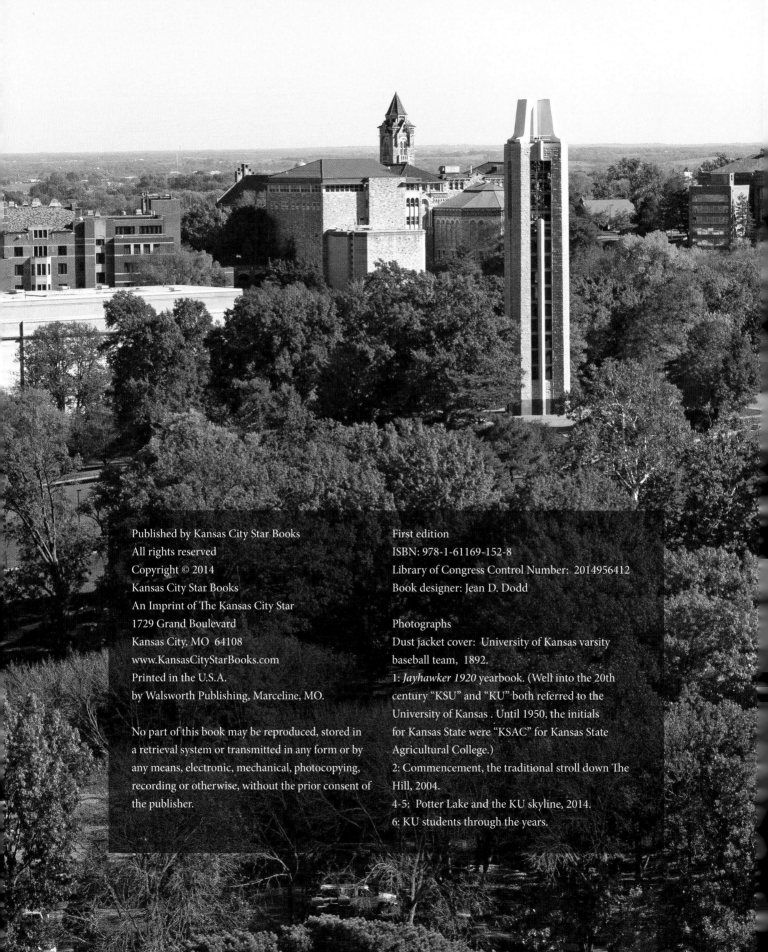

Published by Kansas City Star Books
All rights reserved
Copyright © 2014
Kansas City Star Books
An Imprint of The Kansas City Star
1729 Grand Boulevard
Kansas City, MO 64108
www.KansasCityStarBooks.com
Printed in the U.S.A.
by Walsworth Publishing, Marceline, MO.

First edition
ISBN: 978-1-61169-152-8
Library of Congress Control Number: 2014956412
Book designer: Jean D. Dodd

Photographs
Dust jacket cover: University of Kansas varsity
baseball team, 1892.
1: *Jayhawker 1920* yearbook. (Well into the 20th
century "KSU" and "KU" both referred to the
University of Kansas . Until 1950, the initials
for Kansas State were "KSAC" for Kansas State
Agricultural College.)
2: Commencement, the traditional stroll down The
Hill, 2004.
4-5: Potter Lake and the KU skyline, 2014.
6: KU students through the years.

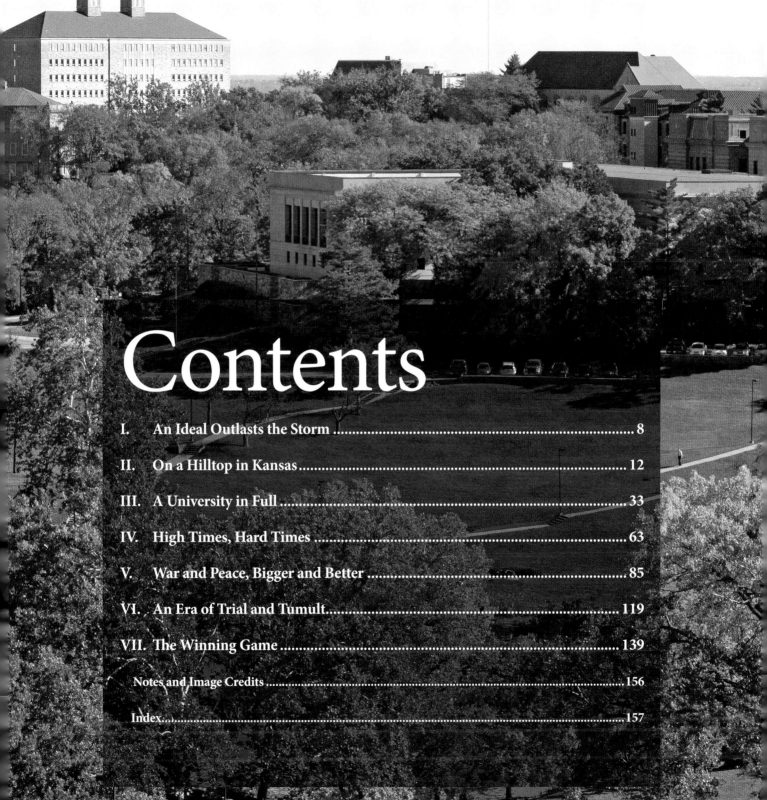

Contents

Foreword

In 1902, the *Jayhawker* yearbook published a brief poem, "A Senior's Wail," illustrated by a woman in cap and gown, her head wistfully in hand.

Would I were a Freshman!
Would I were a Soph!
Would I were a Junior!
Would I were a Prof!

A senior, on the other hand, had to go out in the world, and the poem ended with this lament about graduating:

Would I were most anything!
Could I only stay!

Surely, that captures the thought of many of us who graduated from the University of Kansas. For most students and most alumni, I believe, the years at KU pass too quickly. Look no further than commencement, when we sang the alma mater, swaying from side to side, arms on one another's shoulders, in that sentimental communal dance that unstoppably led to one more rendition of the Rock Chalk Chant.

Every graduate has a different set of memories, but surely most recall a professor or two or three who opened our eyes and our minds to a subject. Decades back, one professor called it "the shock of recognition;" the sudden understanding that showed on a student's face. For the professor, that look made teaching worthwhile. For the students who experienced the "shock," it made class time invaluable.

Many of us will also think of winter nights in Allen Fieldhouse and autumn afternoons at the football stadium, of evenings in the stacks at Watson Library and the trudge across the top of the hill in the windy dead of winter. We'll think of old roommates and friends, college romances, hot political discussions, carousing at the taverns over cold beers and a favorite moment, a favorite passion or a favorite joke.

And there was something else in our years on Mount Oread and its environs: the drop-dead beauty of the place. The Hill is only a bump on the topography of Kansas, but what a job it does! It ties together a collection of buildings whose architecture otherwise ranges from delightful to deadening. It's covered by groves of trees and lines of shrubs laced by streets and sidewalks in a way that seems natural. Early photographs, however, show how it took decades of human intervention to turn a bald hilltop of the 1860s into the landscaped campus of today.

From the top of Mount Oread, you can see a long, long way. The university, as this book shows, has come a long, long way in its first century and a half. So let's get on with the story….

Monroe Dodd
B.S. 1971
M.A. 1974

CHAPTER I

An Ideal Outlasts the Storm

Kansas would have a public university; there was never much doubt about that. In the chaotic 1850s, when pockets of settlers fought and died over whether Kansas would be slave or free, partisans of both stripes wrote into their plans an institution of higher education.

First, however, they had to settle where Kansas stood on the matter that dominated the national debate.

Would Kansas prohibit slavery? The New Englanders and middle westerners who started the communities of Lawrence and Topeka and Manhattan argued fiercely that it would.

As for higher education, the need for a university seemed clear to all. Free-soilers from New England considered higher education a must for a civilized society...

Their heritage and culture and — perhaps most important to them, the God they worshipped — dictated that slavery was an abomination.

Or would Kansas allow it? Pro-slavery Missourians — not many years removed from being Kentuckians and Virginians— who moved to Leavenworth, Atchison and Lecompton considered slavery as much a part of the natural order as the right to own property.

In 1854 the federal government had carved Kansas Territory out of what was called Indian Territory, a place where various tribes were moved from the rapidly filling states in the East. Earlier, the land had been part of the Louisiana Purchase and earlier still, simply a vast chunk of North America inhabited by Native Americans and claimed, but never surveyed or settled, by various colonial powers.

Congress' idea was to organize the country so railroads could build their way west, but immediately it became wrapped up in the great debate. The new Kansas Territory lay above a line of latitude where, according to the Compromise of 1820, slavery was supposed to have been prohibited. To grease the way for congressional approval, officials altered the arrangement: American immigrants to this new territory could decide the slavery question on their own. That infuriated zealous abolitionists, particularly in New England, and inspired pro-slavery ideologues in Missouri and their compatriots in the South.

Beginning in 1854, both sides dispatched legions of people to inhabit the territory and to decide the question. They did so with guns and speeches and occasionally even votes. In the little communities that popped up in the eastern part of Kansas Territory, mayhem and destruction became facts of life. Each side formed its own legislature to write its own constitution, all the while deriding the other side as illegal or bogus.

As for higher education, the need for a university seemed clear to all. Free-soilers from New England considered higher education a must

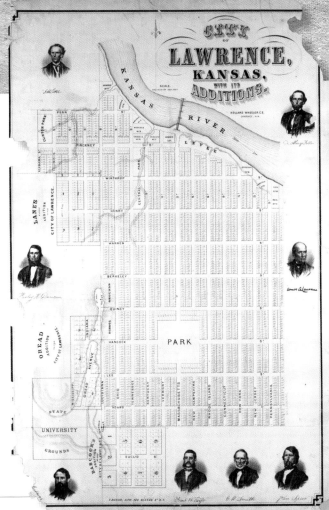

Above, Massachusetts Street in Lawrence, 1863. Right: Lawrence as laid out in the 1850s. The mapmaker designated a spot for the state university.

for a civilized society, and their colleagues from Midwestern states were conscious of the public universities established there. Slaveholding states, too, had long before established their own public universities, among them Virginia, Georgia, Alabama and the nearest state to Kansas Territory, Missouri.

In 1855 a pro-slavery legislature drew up a constitution with a provision for a state educational system, at the top of which would be the University of the Territory of Kansas in Douglas, a few miles up the Kansas River from Lawrence. Free-state partisans convening in Topeka crafted their own constitution, which allowed but did not directly establish a state university. Those efforts went for naught: Congress rejected both constitutions. Other constitutions came and went and nothing came of them.

Finally, in 1859 anti-slavery winds blew stronger. A convention in the city of Wyandotte, which later became part of Kansas City, Kansas, proposed a state constitution that would ban slavery and also establish a state university. Money would come from the sale of land handed over from the federal government and also from grants from the Legislature and private gifts.

Unlike its predecessors, the Wyandotte Constitution won approval in Congress and on January 29, 1861, Kansas came into the Union as a free state. Now, as the United States split into two and the North and South went to war, the scramble began in Kansas for the plums of statehood: the state capital, the state prison and the state university.

For at least five years, the civic leaders of Lawrence had angled to get a college of some kind; a city's reputation, character and future prospects were at stake. But having the university appealed to leaders of other towns, too, particularly Manhattan.

After statehood, Leavenworth entered the picture, but early on settled for the penitentiary. In November 1861 Kansans voted to make Topeka the capital.

The remaining plum was the university, the object of both Lawrence and Manhattan and now Emporia, too. In the end, Kansas divided the plum three ways. Manhattan got an agricultural and mechanical school made possible by passage of the federal Morrill Act,

Charles Robinson

Sara Robinson

under which the national government gave states land to sell and to use the proceeds to teach agricultural and mechanical arts. To appease Emporia, the Legislature granted it the normal school for training teachers.

Lawrence would get the university — if it fulfilled its promise to put up $15,000 and 40 acres of land. In February 1863 the Legislature gave Lawrence until November 1 to make good. The city's leaders soon persuaded Amos Lawrence of Boston to provide $10,000 and they raised the rest through a loan from Governor Thomas Carney. They acquired 40 acres from Carney's predecessor as governor, Charles Robinson, and his wife, Sara Robinson, in return for other property. The land straddled Mount Oread, a ridge that overlooked Lawrence.

Then one August morning

William Quantrill and his band of Missouri-based bushwhackers rode into Lawrence, burned building after building and killed 150 male residents. A thoroughly debilitated Lawrence suddenly faced difficulty repaying its $5,000 loan. In 1864, however, a sympathetic Legislature extinguished the debt and proceeded to approve concrete plans for the university.

It would be headed by its own Board of Regents, whose first meeting would formally represent the beginning of the university. The mission would be to provide Kansans a "thorough knowledge of the various branches of literature, science and the arts."

Money problems and the Civil War delayed the first board's meeting, but a new Board of Regents finally gathered on March 21, 1865. When that day arrived, no professors had been hired, no students enrolled, no building built, and the first classes lay a year and a half in the future. Nevertheless, as the formal date of organization 1865 would be inscribed on the university seal.

In that meeting the regents chose as chancellor an Episcopalian minister from Lawrence, Robert W. Oliver. Unlike later chancellors, Oliver's duties were limited to overseeing finances and presiding at meetings of the regents or their executive committee. To

Robert W. Oliver

run the institution day to day, overseeing faculty and students, would be a yet-unnamed president of the faculty.

The regents tried various strategies for raising money, even tapping private funds donated by well-wishers for the relief of losses suffered by Lawrence in Quantrill's raid. In addition, they pinched pennies. They would construct the new college building on a foundation laid in 1859 on the northern brow of Mount Oread for a denominational college that was never brought into being. The foundation sat

half a mile north of the 40 acres acquired from the Robinsons. So to the university's holdings the regents added acreage containing the unfinished structure.

In September 1865 work got under way. Haltingly at first because of a severe winter, and then picking up speed in March, the building rose at the top of the treeless ridge. By September 1866 it was done. It measured 50 feet on each side and stood three stories high, complete with classrooms, offices, library, assembly hall and chapel. Physically, the University of Kansas amounted to that single building.

The institution also would need someone to teach. The regents turned to the Legislature, which pitched in $7,000 for faculty salaries and equipment, and in July 1866 they hired a faculty of three.

Two of them were new to their profession. David Robinson, in his late 20s and a native of New York, would teach languages and ancient culture. Francis Snow, only 26 and originally from Massachusetts, would teach mathematics and natural sciences. The third member of the first faculty, Elial J. Rice, at 44 was older and more experienced than either of his colleagues, so he was chosen to become the head of instruction in the role of acting president of the faculty.

The junior professors, Robinson and Snow, arrived in Lawrence only weeks before the fall semester began, rented rooms and headed to visit the chancellor.

What did he want them to do? Nothing right away, Oliver replied, advising the young men to get guns and a horse and go hunt prairie chickens and quail.

Surprised at the relaxed attitude yet pleased at the idea of taking several days off to hunt, the young professors did just that. Nine days afterward, the University of Kansas opened its doors.

On a Hilltop in Kansas

At 8:30 a.m. on September 12, 1866, prospective students of the University of Kansas presented themselves at the new building on the hill overlooking Lawrence. They numbered 49, and almost all hailed from Lawrence or from rural Douglas County. The chancellor and faculty were present. So were carpenters, still noisily at work on the stairs.

That afternoon, dedication ceremonies would take place with music by a Lawrence band and rounds of speeches by notables. "The elite of Lawrence was out en masse," wrote *The Kansas Daily Tribune*. "Doctors, lawyers, clergymen, editors, ladies and citizens… were packed into the spacious hall."

Before that, however, the first order of business was for the faculty to interview each student to determine his or her readiness for college work. Quickly, the three professors realized that among the youths were no qualified seniors, nor any qualified juniors. Continuing to test the candidates, the three professors concluded that several of the young people showed promise, but not one was ready for college work.

"We had a few candidates for the lower forms of a rather indifferent high school," David Robinson recalled.

David Robinson, one of three in the first faculty.

Setting the bar high

Because of the dislocations, disruptions and disputatiousness of the Civil War years, Kansas had not developed high schools. The state's first, in Leavenworth, did not open until the same year as the university. Nevertheless, the faculty refused to lower standards.

"We aim to be thorough," wrote another professor, Francis Snow, "even if we don't graduate a student for ten years. You wonder that so few are ready for the college course, but you must remember that our standard is as high as that at Harvard. . . ."

Maintaining those high standards for the college-level curriculum meant that in the university's first year there would be no college curriculum. Instead, the University of Kansas began its life as a preparatory academy. As classwork began, the number of students grew to 55, 29 of them men and 26 women. Courses included Latin, Greek, arithmetic, geography, grammar and history.

Years afterward, Snow would characterize these years as the university's "high school period, with some premonitions of an approaching collegiate character."

David Robinson, too, would acknowledge that this optimistically named university at its

Where it all began: The university's first building, photographed in 1867 by Alexander Gardner.

inception could aspire only to high-school-level work. Yet his hopes remained high, based on what he saw in the character of the Kansans who had endured so much to form a free state.

"I thought then," Robinson recalled a quarter-century later, "and hold the same opinion still, that the superior intelligence and moral purpose of the early settlers must soon show itself in better schools and brighter pupils than are found in the other western states, and eventually equal the best to be found in the older parts of the country."

So it would be a university "in embryonic form," Robinson believed, passing through "the first stage of its endless development."

In that first academic year of 1866-1867, any optimism by the faculty faced a difficult reality. As spring 1867 came around, Robinson recalled, students "gradually disappeared…without sign or warning." By mid-April more than half had

departed. Their departure signaled a fact of life in still-rural America: "Spring work, having opened, most of our brawny students had gone home to assist on the farms."

But home duties weren't the only reason.

"Several in the city, suffering from the usual strain of head-work," Robinson said, "were down with the 'spring-fever,' almost hopeless cases."

The faculty discussed the matter with the young people who remained and with their parents, and persuaded enough to stick around that the first academic year of the University of Kansas closed "triumphantly" with 22 students still on board.

Ready for college work

Undaunted by the defections toward the end of its first academic year, the University of Kansas began its second fall semester in September 1867 with more than 100 students on hand. Two of them, both women, qualified for college-level work.

KU now was a university in fact as well as name — but only barely. As it happened, neither woman would graduate. One, a freshman from Lawrence, quit before finishing. The other, a junior from Olathe named Henrietta Beach, married Professor Robinson. She, too, left school.

Francis Snow

For the students who stuck with it, the complements of education were few. A library existed in name, but it had no books and only a few volumes of congressional records. The first two librarians came from the Board of Regents. They could spare the time because a library with little in the way of holdings required little or no supervision. As late as 1873 the university catalog mentioned that students "are permitted to avail themselves of the private libraries of the Faculty."

As for that faculty, its earliest members had difficulty getting along. Elial Rice, the acting president of the faculty, was said to have put on airs with his two fellow professors, Snow and Robinson. Among the students, Rice developed a reputation for sternness, sometimes to excess. In

"...the superior intelligence and moral purpose of the early settlers must soon show itself in better schools and brighter pupils than are found in the other western states, and eventually equal the best to be found in the older parts of the country."

— *David Robinson*

summer 1867, after teaching only through KU's first academic year, he left for the presidency of Baker University in Baldwin City.

The regents replaced Rice and authorized three new faculty positions — in music, hygiene and French. They filled the jobs quickly, the last with the university's first female professor.

Near the end of 1867, Chancellor Oliver resigned to accept a job with the Episcopal Church in Nebraska. For his work at the university, he had taken no pay. Before replacing him, the regents strengthened the post by folding into its duties the tasks of the faculty president — which had been Elial Rice's responsibility. They came up with three candidates to fill the chancellorship, and in December 1867 narrowed the list to one: John Fraser, formerly president of the Pennsylvania Agricultural College. Fraser accepted their offer.

He arrived in Lawrence in June 1868. One hundred twenty-two students enrolled that fall, six of them in college-level classes. Clearly, the vast majority of students and their parents used the University of Kansas as a high school. From the first, Fraser's job was to create an actual university.

The 41-year-old Fraser was widely experienced and in many ways well-fitted for making something out of very little. He was born and educated in Scotland and had taught briefly in Bermuda and New York City before moving to Pennsylvania. In the Civil War, Fraser led a Union regiment

Elial Rice, soon to exit

that included a company of students from Jefferson College, where he had taught. He rose to colonel and participated in battles at Gettysburg, Chancellorsville and the Wilderness. In mid-1864, he was captured and lived through most of the remainder of the war in Confederate prison camps. Once the war was over, Fraser moved to

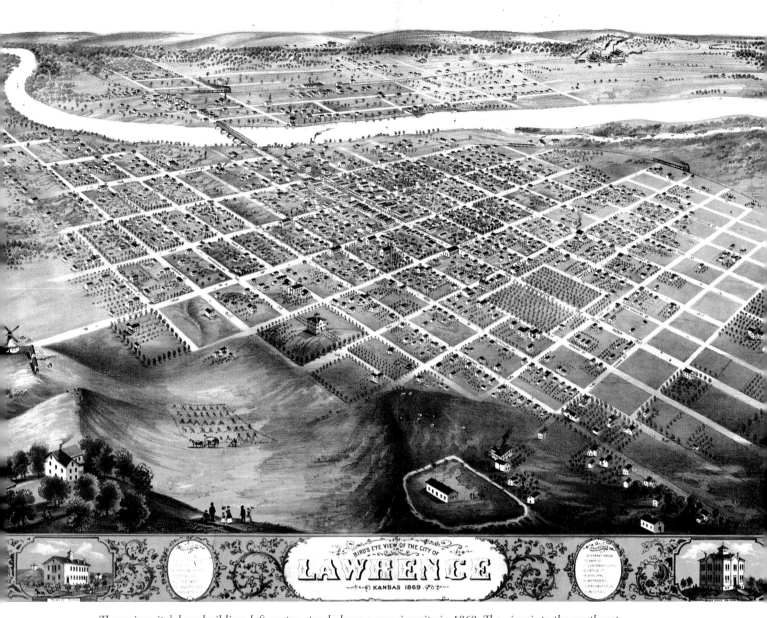

The university's lone building, left center, stood above a growing city in 1869. The view is to the northeast.

the Pennsylvania Agricultural College, becoming its president in 1866.

Fraser's specialty was mathematics, but he also had a command of history, law, natural sciences and literature. Students of Fraser described him as disciplined and indefatigable with expressive eyes and a rich, musical voice. Robinson called the new chancellor a man of "unusual ability and force of character." The ability would serve Fraser well, and so would his force of character — at least for a while.

Setting out his philosophy, Fraser wrote that the university owed it to society to provide youth a broad and diversified education. It should teach science and philosophy and psychology as well as logic and mathematics. It should offer poetry and the social sciences. Literature, he wrote, would fill the "little nooks and corners of society unreachable by history or sermons."

To accomplish all that more faculty would be needed so Fraser added instructors for courses in German and drawing, for anatomy, physiology

The university's college-level students in 1872.

and hygiene, for chemistry and for voice.

Bursting at the seams

With increased faculty and a growing student population, the university naturally would need a bigger building. By fall semester 1869, the institution already had exceeded the capacity of its three-story structure at the northern end of Mount Oread. Some classes spilled over to the basement of Lawrence's Unitarian Church, which stood just down the hill.

John Fraser

The regents agreed with Fraser that the university needed a new building, yet they discouraged him from approaching the Legislature. They spoke from experience. Before Fraser even arrived, the Legislature had turned down the regents' request for $50,000 in bonds to build a second building and also slashed faculty salaries and maintenance money. The university, it turned out, was not universally acclaimed.

"Our enemies," Professor Robinson recalled, without naming them, "only laughed, and said that they knew a high school when they saw one, and we had nothing more. We should not have cared much for these men, had not some of them soon turned up as members of the Legislature. Here they soon became very annoying."

One legislator from Johnson County spoke long and abusively against the expense borne by the state to support the university, saying it had eight to ten times as many professors as it needed. The legislator knew one man, a friend of his, "who, with the aid of his wife, would undertake to teach everything now taught there, and do it better than at present, for the small sum of five hundred dollars a year!"

The offer was not accepted, Robinson recalled, and eventually the same legislator repented and turned to helping the university.

For now, the university's backers turned to the city of Lawrence, asking it to issue $100,000 in bonds with which to construct as many as three more buildings. In February 1870 Lawrence voters approved the idea. Fraser visited colleges in the East to get ideas for the grand expansion, and then set to work overseeing the drawing of plans.

Soon, he and the regents realized they could afford only one new structure. For a fledgling university in a still-new state, however, it would be a magnificent one. The new building would stretch nearly 250 feet north and south, and just short of 100 feet east to west. It would rise four stories and feature three main units separated by twin towers, all in the French Second Empire design popular in the United States at the time. Limestone formed the exterior walls.

Construction began in July 1870. When it became clear that even a single building would outstrip the Lawrence bond issue, university leaders asked the Legislature for $50,000 more. This go-round, the Legislature agreed.

The edifice at first was called simply the University, and then New Building, and then Main Building. Later it was formally named University Hall, and later still it would become Fraser Hall. The building opened for classes December 2, 1872, although it was still shy of completion. Boards covered 22 of its windows and Chancellor Fraser reported that "the cold air of winter finds free ingress." A few more years would pass before requests to the Legislature brought enough money to finish the interior.

Nevertheless, it made a grand home. The structure housed nearly everything there was about the University of Kansas — classrooms, laboratories, offices for administration and faculty, library and a two-floor-tall assembly hall. It stood on the original 40-acre tract acquired by the university, which, though still on sprawling Mount Oread, lay more than half a mile south of

the original building. That building on the northern brow of the ridge, only six years old, was mothballed. It would sit vacant for years. Eventually, the structure was named North College.

The year the new building opened, attendance reached 272 and college-level enrollment numbered 73. At the end of that 1872-1873 academic year, the university conferred degrees on its first true college graduates. Two of them entered the collegiate-level program as freshmen in 1869 and stayed the course for four years. A third man entered as a sophomore in 1870, and in early 1872 a woman transferred into the group.

He and the regents realized they could afford only one new structure, yet for a fledgling university in a still-new state it would be a magnificent one.

KU's first collegiate commencement took place June 11, 1873, in the new building. The valedictorian was Flora Richardson, who in her address figuratively passed the torch to the junior class and symbolized the occasion by literally presenting them an old silk hat. Graduating with her were Lindorf Tosh, Murray Harris and Ralph Collins. After they received diplomas, the university's first four graduates dined at a banquet in their honor in the new building's auditorium attended by townspeople, state officials and even a group of Congregationalist clergy in town for a convention.

According to legend, during the banquet some pranksters lowered from the open ceiling of the assembly hall a skeleton bearing a card that read "Prex." Fraser's wife asked him what it meant, and he replied, "The faculty."

The main commencement address sounded a more dignified note. In it, Senator John J. Ingalls of Kansas marveled at the material growth of Kansas in so short a time, and also at "those higher attributes" expressed in the commencement itself.

"This," he declared, "is the State's consummate hour."

New powers, but more disputes

Combining the jobs of chancellor and faculty president gave Fraser considerably more power than Oliver

The university's proud new building in 1873.

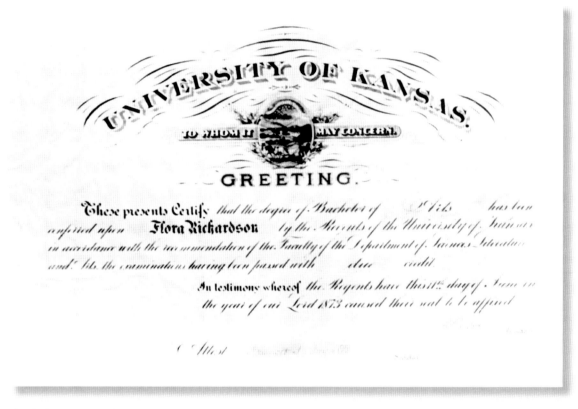

The diploma awarded in 1873 to the valedictorian of the first graduating class, Flora Richardson.

had enjoyed, and shortly after his arrival Fraser succeeded in strengthening the office even further. Under new rules adopted by the regents in January 1869, the chancellor would serve not only as chair of the faculty and a member of the regents, but also as the board's chief executive.

Faculty members were to enforce the rules set by the regents and receive "free and equal voice" in deliberations about internal management. They were encouraged to share ideas about teaching and to train their students in "habits of independent observation and research."

The faculty continued to increase in number and so did the range of courses offered by the university. Added were a professorship of modern languages, and of mathematics. Then came a position in history, English language and literature, and one of physics and another

of general and industrial drawing. Sometimes new faculty members added courses to their own portfolios; the professor of general and industrial drawing, who was a civil engineer, also taught surveying, topography and applied mechanics.

In Fraser's six years as chancellor the university grew handsomely. With that success, however, friction grew between the chancellor and faculty members. One critic described Fraser as hot-tempered and unwilling to brook criticism. At a faculty meeting in fall 1874, the chancellor and a professor exchanged heated words over the head count of students listed in the annual catalog.

Even an admirer wrote that Fraser, in dealing with faculty, acted too much like the former Union Army officer he was, with military rigidity. Another writer called him "devoid of

When world views collided

Disputes between faculty and administrators probably are inevitable at any institution: Nimble brains, academic resumes and ample egos can run up against one another. Add religion and questions about the proper roles of men and women, and the mixture can become volatile, as happened in the case of Kate Stephens in the 1880s.

Stephens entered the preparatory school in 1868 and graduated from the university's college-level courses in 1875. She studied Greek intensively, received a master's degree in 1878 and in June of that year joined the faculty. In 1879, she became a full professor at the age of 26.

Kate Stephens, who spoke her mind.

Unlike the chancellors of the era and most of the regents, she belonged to no denomination and professed no religion, choosing instead, she said, to respect the virtues of spirit, beauty and mind. She spoke out whenever she wanted and firmly believed all her ideas were correct.

Her students considered her a wonderful teacher. Her chancellor, Joshua Lippincott, probably considered her a pain in the neck.

The firing of James Marvin, chancellor when she was hired, outraged her. She lost no love for Marvin's successor, Lippincott. In 1885, she produced a departmental report to the Board of Regents that called Lippincott "your representative in the faculty," reducing the chancellor to a mere functionary of the regents. To ensure that her opinion was not mistaken, she referred to James Marvin as the "former President and honorable Chancellor."

In the same report, Stephens scathed the "Philistine materialism" she found all around, along with the "pettiness of social and political rival factions."

The Board of Regents and Governor George Glick, of course, represented one such faction.

Voting unanimously, and giving no reason publicly, the regents declared her insubordinate and in April 1885 sent word that her services were no longer needed. In the wake of her firing, Stephens told a newspaper reporter that administrators simply had no use for outspoken female faculty members. Also, she suspected her lack of professed religious convictions played a part.

There may have been another reason. It happened that Stephens' late father — a Lawrence judge who had been an important force behind the establishment of the university Law Department in 1878 — had once entered a judgment against one of the regents. The regent may have taken out his grievance on the judge's daughter. More than two decades later, one of the regents who had voted to fire her told her that her father's action was, in fact, the reason. Stephens moved to the East, where she became an editor for several publishing houses.

From time to time, she returned to Lawrence to make speeches supporting women's rights and suffrage. She also campaigned for women to be appointed to the Board of Regents.

In the 1920s, believing that her father's role in the establishment of the law school had been diminished by the longtime dean, James Green, she wrote a book challenging Green's own accomplishments. Complicating matters was the fact that Green was Stephens' brother-in-law.

Kate Stephens eventually moved back to Lawrence and died in 1938.

political sensibility."

The result was that Fraser proved unable to harmonize or at least to comfort competing interests and ambitions. One group of faculty took its complaints to the regents.

At the same time, the regents were reconstituted from 12 members to six. Among the six, Fraser had antagonists. Between that and the faculty uprising, his future as chancellor began to dim, and the fact was made clear to him. In time, the regents and Fraser reached an accommodation: He would step down if the regents supported him for election as state superintendent of education. It was agreed, and in April 1874 Fraser resigned.

That fall, the Republican party nominated Fraser for the Kansas education post and he won election, serving two years before moving to a college job in Pennsylvania. Not until more than two decades later would the university recognize his handiwork. In 1897, the grand new home for the university that he had pushed into being was named Fraser Hall.

The regents' first attempt to replace Fraser misfired. They chose a University of Wisconsin faculty member, Stephen H. Carpenter, based on his resume. Carpenter accepted the job and traveled to Lawrence to begin work. Arriving in August 1874, he found Kansas in the middle of a 100-degree heat wave, a drought and a grasshopper plague. Without setting foot on campus, he turned around, returned to cooler Wisconsin and wrote the regents that he was declining the position.

In November the regents turned to James Marvin, a mathematics professor at Allegheny College in Pennsylvania. Marvin, who turned 54 that year, was born in New York and had served as a superintendent of

Rock Chalk!

Today, crowds sound out the rock chalk chant at the beginning of football and basketball games, and — if the basketball team is headed for a victory — toward the end, too. The chant also forms part of the closing ceremonies at commencement. Generations of students have intoned it and generations of alumni recognize it.

For all of the chant's use in front of tens of thousands of people, it began on a much smaller scale, not as an encouragement for athletic teams but as a bonding mechanism for the University Science Club. At one of the club's weekly meetings in spring 1886, according to Robert Taft in his *The Years on Mount Oread*, some member remarked that the club needed a yell. Professor E.H.S. Bailey of the Chemistry Department suggested: "Rah, Rah, Jay Hawk, K-S-U." In those days, shorthand for the University of Kansas was often "KSU" in addition to "KU" — perhaps because the former worked better rhythmically. "Jay Hawk," or "Jayhawk" stemmed from longtime usage, memorably by soldiers of fortune who aligned with the free-state side in territorial days.

College War Cries.

Every college of importance in this country has a college cry. In every town in which a college is situated, the midnight air resounds with the hideous yells of the student symbolic of victory, defeat, or devilment. The student of University of Kansas use their yell but little and it is only amidst great victory that Rock-chalk-Jay-hawk, K-U-U-U float through the midnight air reminding one of a band of Apache Indians.

Repeated three times in staccato, Bailey's yell caught on. In the 1886-1887 academic year, someone suggested "Rock Chalk" would sound crisper then "Rah, Rah." Mount Oread had limestone outcroppings that could be mistaken for chalk rock, so the story goes, and western Kansas contains formations of the actual mineral.

A student newspaper, *The Weekly University Courier*, had for some time advocated creation of a university yell, and in advance of a state oratorical contest in February 1887 it printed the Science Club version as "Rock-Chock-Jay Hawk-K.U." In November 1887, it corrected the spelling to "Rock-chalk" and printed the acronym at the end as "K-U-U-U," suggesting a drawn-out note.

The current version, with two slow repetitions followed by three staccato rounds, evidently was in place by 1889. Supposedly hailed by Theodore Roosevelt as the greatest college cheer, the chant has stuck through time.

Faculty for the 1881-1882 academic year included Chancellor Marvin, center, and two original faculty members in the second row, Francis Snow at left and David Robinson, second from right.

schools in Ohio. In addition, he was a Methodist minister.

He accepted the position and, to the regents' relief, showed up for work. Yet work would not be easy.

Hard times

On commencement day 1873, the one that Senator Ingalls proclaimed as the state's consummate hour, no one suspected that darker hours lay just around the corner. Later that year, a financial crisis brought on by over-exuberant investment in postwar railroads helped cause an economic recession across America. Worried depositors withdrew money from banks, credit tightened, the railroad expansion cooled, bringing down steel and other industries that supplied the boom, and workers lost jobs. In Kansas, long periods of drought and plagues of grasshoppers added to the misery of farmers, and thus to the misery of the state economy. Kansans tightened up their spending, and expected state government to do the same. As the Legislature reined in appropriations the financial crisis rippled into the university budget.

James Marvin

The new chancellor and the regents navigated as best they could. Cuts came in the faculty payroll — which led to dismissals and resignations — and in funds for the library. The university put off finishing the interior of the Main Building. In 1875, Marvin's own pay was chopped from $3,000 a year to $2,000.

Aside from whatever money the university could persuade the Legislature to provide, Marvin and the board had few places to turn. The 72 square miles of federal land handed over when the university opened had brought lower prices than hoped, and so their sale generated less income than expected. Private gifts were few

Lilac bushes, planted as part of an 1870s campus beautification project, towered over visitors in the 1910s.

and small, and tuition provided little help. The university charged fees only to students in certain specialty areas such as music, medicine and law.

In the 1874-1875 state fiscal year, which in those days began and ended in November, the regents received $20,000 to spend on the university. All except $2,000 came from the Legislature. The next year, still chopping away at requests for money, the Legislature reduced the budget for teacher education at Emporia and ordered KU to establish its own education department — without providing any extra money for it. The university opened its "normal" or teacher training department in 1876. The program would survive until 1885, when the regents shut it down, and then would be revived early in the 20th century.

A story that became part of early KU lore has the chancellor and the governor walking through University Hall on some ceremonial occasion. The governor noticed that a stairway handrail, most of which was made of hardwood, had been finished with a length of unstained pine and asked what happened.

The university as idea

In the 1970s, Clifford Griffin, a member of the KU history faculty who specialized in intellectual history, explored a central question faced by all of those who led the University of Kansas, and particularly its early leaders: Just what was a public university supposed to be?

In the late 19th century, what it was not was a traditional private college, which existed to teach mainly the liberal arts. Supporters of the university believed it should try to keep up with, and even ahead of, the growth of the country by stressing research and by instituting professional schools. Yet, as Griffin writes in his 1974 book, *The University of Kansas: A History,* questions remained.

Should the university be universal in its academic offerings? Should it concentrate its effort on research for research's sake? Should it concentrate on public service, a direction that would prove useful in gaining support from its constituents?

As chancellor, James Marvin leaned toward the ideal of universality. To him, a university ought to serve its students in any way that prepared them for life. Marvin's successor, Joshua Lippincott, added to that an emphasis on research, and on the university as a stronghold of knowledge. Lippincott thought the university should be a key part of the public educational system. Lippincott's successor, Francis Snow, agreed and also stressed academic freedom and adaptation to the needs of Kansas — not of some model in the East.

Lippincott and Snow agreed that reaching the ideal probably was unattainable, so they and Marvin struggled to polish their definition.

"The University of Kansas," Griffin wrote, "continued to be eminently pragmatic and experimental."

One matter was not in dispute: the university would be a moral place as defined by the Christian tradition, which dominated American thinking in the late 19th century. Chancellors Marvin and Lippincott both had been Methodist clergymen at one point in their careers, and Snow had considered becoming one. Those chancellors reassured parents that the university upheld Christian ideals — even if it was not a religious-based institution.

Griffin pointed to one other motive: Higher education prepared people for life at higher status and higher income.

"The common-school work is a sort of hand-to-mouth regime," faculty member James Canfield said. Higher education, on the other hand, can ensure that its graduates have "a surplus of information and intellectual training for emergencies," along with a pool from which future leaders could be drawn.

"That, Governor," Marvin is said to have replied, "is where the money ran out."

In 1876, a strong lobbying effort by regents, faculty and residents of Lawrence won $15,000 from the Legislature to finish the interior. In November 1877, the structure finally was dedicated and named University Hall. By then, the university counted well more than 230 students.

In two areas that did not require large amounts of money, Marvin accomplished much. For one, he restored decent relations between chancellor and faculty and harmony among competing faculty interests. For another, he greatly improved the surroundings.

From the university's earliest days, Mount Oread had been a starkly barren place badly in need of landscaping. In 1877, at Marvin's urging, the regents eked out of the Legislature $1,200 for hedges and fencing, and for a stone fence and iron gate to form an entrance to campus.

Chancellor Marvin campaigned with the Douglas County Horticultural Society to help beautify the place, and society members and nurserymen donated hundreds of trees — elm, ash, box elder, maple, pine and cedar. On March 29, 1878, the first Arbor Day in Lawrence, Marvin proclaimed a school holiday and set students to work planting trees. Groups of students competed among themselves to see who could plant the

KU found new uses for its original building in 1890. Law students and fine arts students shared the space.

most. Marvin himself helped placed walnut seeds in the hollow down the hill northwest of the Main Building. One hundred thirty trees sprang from that effort. In 1906, the Board of Regents would name the area Marvin Grove.

Coursework evolves

Although they attended a place that called itself a university, students of the 1860s and 1870s faced a less-than-universal menu. College-level work was divided into only three courses: Classical, Scientific and Modern Literature. Once a student chose his or her course, the classwork went according to a strict plan. Students in the

Classical track studied Latin, Greek, English composition and a variety of other courses in mathematics and the sciences. As they advanced, they moved into literature, more sciences and history. In the Scientific course, French and German took the place of the ancient languages, and courses in drawing and higher math were added. Eventually, Scientific-course students could branch into civil engineering, natural history or chemistry. Modern Literature covered French and German, and various mathematics and science courses along with expanded study of history.

Students encouraged the university to

offer more choices, or electives, so they could tailor their educations to their own talents and expectations for their lives. Faculty studied the question and by early 1880 decided to allow juniors and seniors to choose two subjects each semester on their own from a range of courses. Freshmen and sophomores remained under the old rules of Classical, Scientific or Modern Literature.

By the end of the 1880s, upperclassmen were free to choose any courses they wanted —within 15 majors, or groups of courses, devised by the faculty. Also required were minors, or smaller groupings of courses. Administrators and faculty pronounced the new ways a success. Those changes took place within the university's largest division, called Science, Literature and the Arts. As the years passed and the university evolved, other departments sprang up, offering different educational goals and requiring different entrance requirements.

The Normal Department, ordered into being by the Legislature of 1876 to train teachers, was the first outside Science, Literature and the Arts. The new department at first required only three years of classes, and then shifted to a four-year program by the mid-1880s.

In 1878, a Law Department opened under the leadership of a part-time dean, James W. Green. He was made full-time in the 1880s and was joined by two other professors. When it opened, the Law Department did not require a high school diploma for entrance, only a basic examination in English and history.

A Medical Department opened in 1880, but offered only one year of study. In 1885, Kansas created a state Board of Pharmacy and the university instituted a pharmacy discipline. A degree in pharmacy required two years of study.

Engineering classes had been offered at the university since 1873. Ten years later, the program was expanded with a full professorial chair, filled by Frank Marvin, son of the chancellor. As

engineering courses multiplied, a degree required less and less of the regular coursework offered in Science, Literature and the Arts.

When the university opened, music and art had been minor players; in the 1880s they took on greater importance. By 1884, the regents had authorized a Department of Music, headed by a dean paid partly from the general fund and partly from his students' fees. The middle 1880s also brought an expansion in coursework in the visual arts. By 1890 two art instructors were teaching 40 students.

Better days

In the 1880s, better economic times returned to the country and to Kansas. At the University of Kansas, the financial pinch eased. Faculty numbers rose and so did enrollment. Over the next nine years, until the end of Marvin's tenure, the faculty rose from 10 to 19 members and enrollment grew to several hundred.

Early in the decade, KU got money to build another educational structure, this one dedicated to the use of a single department, Chemistry. Since the opening of University Hall, the chemistry laboratories in the basement had at least annoyed faculty and students in all the other departments on the floors above, and possibly caused health problems undetected by the technology of the era.

"The Chemical Laboratory, under three stories of recitation-rooms," said the student-run *Kansas Review*, "sends its noxious gases into the Department of Physics, corroding the delicate instruments there, into the Library, damaging the bindings of the books, into the Natural History Department, attacking the colors of the numerous fine specimens."

In 1883, the regents directed $12,000 toward a structure that would house the offending laboratories. Work moved quickly and by the end of that year, Professor Edgar H.S. Bailey and his 35 chemistry students moved into their new academic home. The two-story structure, which sat about 50 feet southwest of University Hall, was faced in limestone and brick. Bailey pronounced it as good for its purpose as any west of the Mississippi.

Getting money for any new building symbolized a triumph for the administration of James Marvin, but Marvin would not celebrate for long. State universities are vulnerable to changes in the political wind, and such a change took place in Kansas in 1883.

For the first time in the 22 years of statehood, a Democrat, George Washington Glick, was elected governor, and he named a new Board of Regents. Like Glick, they were Democrats and anti-temperance. Chancellor Marvin was a Republican and pro-temperance to boot.

After long arguments over Marvin's attempt to remove a chemistry professor whose views on politics and religion Marvin did not share, the new regents tired of the chancellor. They brought in a professor from Michigan to interview for

The Chemistry Building, opened in the 1880s.

job — while Marvin still sat in the chancellor's chair. That insulting move infuriated Marvin, and on June 5, 1883, he resigned. The regents

When presidents took in the view

Early in the life of KU, two presidents of the United States came calling. Both rode to the top of Mount Oread and one ascended to the highest point of University Hall to look over the Kansas and Wakarusa valleys.

On April 26, 1873, Ulysses Grant came to town with his wife and daughter on his way west to Colorado. The visit, a last-minute stop, went off with no handshaking or speeches. The carriages of the presidential procession stopped only briefly on campus. Within two hours Grant was back on his train.

In late September 1879, Ruther-ford B. Hayes toured Kansas with his wife, Lucy Hayes, and General William Tecumseh Sherman of Civil War fame. On the way east by train the presidential party stopped September 27 in Lawrence. In open carriages, the group rode from the Kansas Pacific depot down Massachusetts Street under a triumphal arch built for the occasion. Crowds lined the street, and a "constant stream of people," according to *The Lawrence Daily Journal*, filed up Mount Oread in hopes of catching sight of the president when he got there.

Hayes, his wife and Sherman climbed to the observation platform atop University Hall, the president having to persuade Mrs. Hayes by telling her she would regret not seeing the view. After descending the president spoke and students broke into the song, "Marching Through Georgia," in honor of Sherman, who also spoke. From Lawrence, the presidential train headed east to Leavenworth.

Campus visitors followed the president's footsteps; from 1884 to 1886 alone, more than 8,000 signed a guest book kept at the building.

accepted the resignation in late August. Marvin went on to head Haskell Indian Institute and then assumed pastorship of First Methodist Church in Lawrence.

In his place, the regents elected Joshua Lippincott, a native of New Jersey who had served as a high school principal in Pennsylvania and New Jersey and most recently as a mathematics professor at Dickinson College in Pennsylvania. He began his duties as chancellor in September 1883. Like Marvin, Lippincott, who was 48 when he was chosen chancellor, had been a Methodist minister before turning to academe and from time to time he gave sermons in Lawrence churches.

Considered rather grim by his contemporaries and by students, Lippincott nevertheless proved earnest. Working in his favor was the return to health of state and national economies. Appropriations flowed readily from the Legislature.

New buildings and the end of the "high school"

In 1885, two years into Lippincott's tenure, longtime Professor Francis Snow helped persuade the Legislature to come up with $50,000 for another new campus building, this one to house not only science students in his Natural History Department but also Snow's vast collection of insect and other specimens, which surpassed 100,000.

Joshua Lippincott

"The extensive collections are of practical value to the agricultural and horticultural interests of the state," Snow said, clearly tailoring his argument to what legislators' constituents would want to hear. The collections would help "in the determination of the names and habits of our insects, friends and foes." Snow enjoyed

Snow Hall stood west of University Hall.

considerable support from the rest of the faculty for his new structure, at least partly because the collection had consumed increasing amounts of space in University Hall.

The new structure was named Snow Hall. When the governor signed the measure into law on March 6, 1885, along with a general appropriations bill for the university that had undergone few cuts, a celebration erupted in Lawrence. Buoyed by the happy financial news, faculty, students and alumni formed a torchlight parade, and Snow rode on the shoulders of four students to a platform downtown.

There, Chancellor Lippincott signaled that the legislation marked a new day. The state's generosity, he said, meant that the university no longer amounted to what its critics had called "Lawrence University." Now, Lippincott said, it truly had become "the University of Kansas and we are proud of it."

The Snow Hall of Natural History, built west of University Hall, was dedicated November 16, 1886. It housed not only Snow's enormous collection of specimens, but also classrooms and laboratories.

It was also in Lippincott's tenure that

Student life and diversions

A century and a half ago, a University of Kansas student left home or a Lawrence boarding house each school day, trudged up Mount Oread and entered a single building. In it, he or she joined all the other university students of the time for all the classes there were.

Most early students had grown up in Lawrence; they and their parents were full-fledged townspeople. It's small wonder, as one professor later wrote, that there was little split in those days between town and gown.

As more out-of-town and college-level students enrolled, the "townies" occasionally complained. One wrote *The Kansas Tribune* in 1874 that students on their way to class plucked flowers from bushes and fruit from trees along the way. Sometimes, full-fledged pranks were played on townspeople: here a buggy appeared overnight on a front porch and there a bell sounded in the wee hours of the morning.

Meanwhile, the university listed in the catalog fewer and fewer rules for student behavior. By 1873, it called only for "unexceptional deportment."

Behaving unexceptionally, however, had always been difficult for some students. At KU's 25th anniversary, Professor Arthur G. Canfield wrote that the balance between men and women held down the worst behavior, the "boisterous sorts of fun making."

Groups often associated with boisterous fun-making, fraternities, did not maintain their own living and eating houses in the early years. Members gathered at a rented room for chapter meetings and otherwise lived apart.

The first fraternity appeared in 1873, Beta Thea Pi. The first sorority, I.C. Sorosis, first met the same year. In 1888, it changed to a Greek-letter name, Pi Beta Phi.

Quickly, fraternity and sorority membership grew, along with the number of Greek organizations. By 1891, six fraternities and three sororities claimed about a hundred of the 221 undergraduate students. None maintained fulltime houses until the middle 1890s. To that point, members boarded where they could and met in rented rooms.

So did literary and debating societies, which began the first year, 1866, but declined in late 1880s, the victims of political maneuvering for control that often made winning office more important than debate itself. Also specialty clubs sprang up: a natural history club and clubs for the normal department, law, civil engineering, science, modern languages, pharmacy, history and political sicence. Few musical groups formed in the first 25 years although soon there would be a glee club, mandolin club, band and orchestra.

the Legislature agreed to provide a consistent appropriation of $75,000 a year to the university. The money, delivered in a lump sum, would be parceled out by the regents. The previous method required the regents to recommend specific

To keep that support flowing, Lippincott enlisted the help of alumni. He asked them to boost the university in whatever ways they could, by word or by money, and to answer any criticisms they heard in their communities.

money for certain categories; the Legislature than considered each category, altering each amount as it wanted.

To keep that support flowing, Lippincott

enlisted the help of alumni. He asked them to boost the university in whatever ways they could, by word or by money, and to answer any criticisms they heard in their communities. The university's future, he said, was tied to the "loyalty and zeal of its alumni." On campus, faculty grew in number, as did students.

By 1887, enrollment approached 500 students, and two-thirds of them did college-level work. Gradually, the presence of the preparatory program diminished. It had proved a necessity when so few Kansas youth were prepared for college but by the late 1880s towns across Kansas were developing qualified high schools. Lippincott moved to shut down the department, and his effort fell on willing ears among the faculty and among the regents, where sentiment had built even before Lippincott arrived. In

Natural history courses taught by Francis Snow, far right with net, extended to field trips to the Colorado mountains. This group contained a future general, governor and college faculty members. At far left stood William Allen White, who never finished college but who would win a Pulitzer prize in journalism.

1888, Lippincott proposed to stop admitting preparatory students after June 1889 and to close the department once all its students had departed. From then on, young men and women would be admitted only if they had graduated from a high school accredited by university representatives, or had passed an examination. The regents approved.

On February 28, 1889, Joshua Lippincott resigned after six years as chancellor, telling the regents he thought the ministry suited him better. As it happened, the Legislature had proved difficult that year, one member accusing the chancellor of shirking work, and had cut appropriations. Lippincott took over the pulpit at the First Methodist Church in Topeka. From there, he returned to the East Coast.

In his tenure, faculty increased to nearly 40, Snow Hall was built, and the Department of Pharmacy and an art department established.

Perhaps a hint of the problem that faced Lippincott occurred in an interview given by Senator Ingalls. Praising Lippincott for his work, he nevertheless suggested it was time to look beyond clergymen or former clergymen for the next chancellor. Instead, he encouraged the regents to find "a man trained and skilled in practical affairs" — an expert in public relations, perhaps, or a lawyer.

Lippincott departed KU after commencement in June 1889. For a year, the office would remain unfilled.

A University in Full

As the institution atop Mount Oread finished its first quarter-century of existence, it became what the founders envisioned: a true university for Kansas.

The preparatory department, which had long given critics the chance to deride the university as a "high school," closed, a small but clear signal of KU's development. From then on, true high schools would prepare youth for college-level work. Having shed itself of what one chancellor derided as a "posterior appendage," the University of Kansas in the 1890s embarked on expanding things at the college level.

"We have here a great institution of learning," *The University Weekly Courier* said in 1891. "No more rudimentary instruction, no more narrow restriction to arbitrary courses.... Everything is on a high, a grand and an advanced order."

Furthering that advanced order, law, engineering, pharmacy and fine arts were transformed from departments into full-fledged schools within the university with their own deans. The Department of Science, Literature and the Arts became the College of Arts, later renamed the College of Liberal Arts and Sciences. Within a few years, the university established a graduate school, and then a program leading to the Ph.D. With that, KU offered the highest degree in American education.

Central to the expansion was the library,

Room to research: Spooner's reference division.

Spooner Library relieved a space crunch.

which, when the 1890s began, could barely squeeze its small but growing collection into its longtime home in University Hall. So up went the library's first stand-alone structure, a Romanesque stone building. To the south of University Hall, which in 1897 would be renamed Fraser after the second chancellor, rose a new building for physics and, to the west, one for engineering. Physics became Blake in 1898, named for the professor whose efforts led to its construction. From the first, the engineering building was named Fowler Shops.

Those were only the beginning. The turn of the century would bring yet more structures, built along the east-west axis of Mount Oread to house an increasing body of courses, faculty and students.

Study and research formed the heart of the institution but, in American higher education, identity proved equally important. The late 1880s

A well-outfitted student room of the early 1890s. The men outlined the mirror with portraits of women.

had brought the "Rock Chalk" yell, which caught on quickly and served the fiercely competitive "literary" teams of the era, oratory and debate. Those teams, along with rival student newspapers, created outlets for youthful energy and answered a human need to belong. They did so, however, mostly for the students who participated in them.

Schoolwide allegiance, pride and spirit awaited the arrival of intercollegiate sports, particularly ones whose seasons fell within the academic year. In 1890 students and faculty organized a team to play the rough-and-tumble game of football, a new sport that stirred passions across campus like nothing before. The university team's need for identifying marks would lead to a permanent set of school colors, providing a lasting image for students and alumni. And toward the end of the 1890s, a new physical education instructor would arrive on campus, bringing with him a game he had invented to while away long winter hours, and one in which KU would achieve its greatest athletic glories.

In the years around the turn of the century new studies, new structures and a new spirit rose almost as one. Overseeing it all was a man who had literally seen it all — Francis Huntington Snow. Under his leadership, by measures both real and symbolic, KU met and surpassed even its founders' dreams.

On the hill from the start

The departure of Joshua Lippincott in mid-1899 left the university without a chancellor for more than a year, although the regents busily considered candidates throughout that time. One professor eminently qualified to become chancellor, James Canfield, made too many enemies by advocating free trade. Most Kansans

The campus about 1900 with streets unpaved.

Dressed to the nines, the women of Kappa Kappa Gamma sorority sat for their 1891 group portrait.

of that day supported a strict tariff to discourage imports of foreign goods, among which might be agricultural products that would compete against the state's own crops. Instead, the regents turned in March 1890 to another candidate, a Congregationalist minister from Minneapolis named Charles Thwing who had written a book about colleges. Within days, however, Thwing turned down the job.

The regents then settled on a man who, as part of the university's first faculty, had been present on the university's opening day and had taught at KU ever since. Francis Huntington Snow accepted their offer.

When Snow signed up to teach at the fledgling university in 1866, he was only 26 years old. He hailed from Fitchburg, Massachusetts, where his family had been friends with a leader of the early Kansas settlers, Charles Robinson. From Lawrence, Robinson wrote the young Snow that he believed the regents were likely to hire him to teach. They did, but not for the job Snow sought, teaching languages. Instead, they assigned the young professor to mathematics and natural sciences. Snow would not regret the switch.

Fifty years old the year he became chancellor, Snow had watched KU's first quarter-century unfold — from its first year as a preparatory school with 55 students and three faculty to an institution 10 times that size. As full-time professor of natural history since 1870, he had led expeditions through the American West in search of rare insects, birds, reptiles and plants. Among natural scientists, Snow had become a world-renowned expert. His collection of insects grew to enormous size and he also created collections of other animals and of plants. The production of top scientists from among his students bolstered his reputation. So did the future governors, generals and authors

Francis Snow as Chancellor.

who, whatever their career inclination, had been drawn to Snow's classes.

Besides his accomplishments in teaching and research, Snow had helped persuade legislators to build a separate structure for the natural sciences, a building that had already been named Snow Hall. In 1878, Snow had persuaded his uncle, William B. Spooner of Boston, to leave a substantial sum of his estate to KU. Spooner died in 1880, but legal matters were not resolved

The indomitable librarian

Like the library she oversaw for more than three decades, Carrie M. Watson grew into an institution at the University of Kansas.

Her time in Kansas began in territorial days, when as a small child her family moved there from New York. She went through the university's preparatory program, completed her college degree and served as an assistant to the part-time librarian until 1887, when at 29 she was hired as the first full-time librarian.

With no formal training in librarianship but an avid interest in books, Watson took on the task of improving and enlarging a library, housed in University Hall and universally described as inadequate. She recalled it as "a single small room in the home economics department." Watson possessed no end of determination, and under her leadership the library grew. So did her reputation as a strict disciplinarian whose glare alone could stifle unruliness in her domain.

Carrie Watson

In her tenure, which would last 34 years, Watson presided over a collection that kept overwhelming its space. When room ran out in University Hall, the university built Spooner Library. When that building opened in 1894, the library contained 20,000 volumes and enough space to hold 100,000. Under Watson, even Spooner eventually proved too small.

She loved to read and encouraged the habit in others. Many students recalled Watson fondly, among them the journalist and author William Allen White. As a student, White had suffered rebukes from Watson, but found the book collection invaluable.

"Whatever I got in the way of education," he said years later, "was out of that library."

Yet Watson was not universally admired. Some students found her too stern and controlling, and some professors complained that the library was mismanaged and indifferent to their needs. Watson kept going until 1921, when her health took a turn for the worse and she resigned.

As construction began on a new library in 1923 Watson's critics lost out to her supporters, among them White and Governor Jonathan M. Davis, also a former student. With their support, the new structure was named for her. She died at her home in Lawrence in 1943.

until 1891. That year — Francis Snow's first full calendar year as chancellor — the university received more than $91,000 from Spooner's estate, which was to be used for the new library building.

The regents elected Francis Snow chancellor on April 11, 1890. The choice met widespread praise. Students paraded to Snow's house and then downtown. The next night, the faculty dropped in at the Snow residence to entertain and make speeches of support. Talking and singing lasted to a late hour.

Snow was inaugurated June 11, 1890, taking over an institution with an enrollment of 505 students and 34 faculty. In his inaugural address, Snow called for more research tools such as laboratories, apparatus and books. He also urged the Legislature to spend more money on salaries, aiming to keep KU's best faculty and even hire good faculty from older universities. And he sought to reduce the teaching load.

Meanwhile, a reorganization of the university got under way. The faculty, administration and regents drew up a plan creating schools, each with a dean. It also created a University Council, composed of the chancellor and the deans, to advise the chancellor and to administer student discipline and it established the office of registrar to oversee admissions and student records. According to Clifford Griffin in his *The University of Kansas: A History,* the move had the effect of limiting faculty knowledge of university doings; before the reorganization, the faculty as a whole met with the chancellor. Afterward, they met as schools. As a result, the chancellor became the single office with a hand in every part of the university.

The first departments transformed into schools were law and pharmacy in 1890. The department heads, James W. Green in law and Lucius E. Sayre in pharmacy, continued as leaders with the title of dean. Law and its 56

The newly installed chancellor, Francis Snow, in his office at University Hall with his secretary, Vernon Kellogg.

students moved out of University Hall to KU's original building at the northern end of Mount Oread. Now known as Old North College, the building had stood vacant for years, except for a few years in which it was used as a rest home. In 1896, the Law School would expand to a three-year program.

Also in 1891, at the request of the faculty, the civil and electrical engineering programs were elevated to become the School of Engineering. Frank O. Marvin, who had been at KU since 1878 and was the son of former Chancellor James

Marvin had grand visions for his students and graduates. He saw engineers as professionals, influential future citizens fitted with "large responsibility concerned with public works."

Marvin, was made dean. Soon the school added new disciplines: chemical engineering, hydraulic

engineering and, toward the end of the 1890s, mechanical and mining engineering. Marvin had grand visions for his students and graduates. He saw engineers as professionals, influential future citizens fitted with "large responsibility concerned with public works." He also wanted his engineers to have an appreciation of art and music, and thereby bring to their work "an artistic quality."

In 1892, the music and fine arts programs were combined into a School of Music and Painting. The dean was the existing leader, George B. Penny, who was succeeded in 1893 by Charles S. Skilton. In 1894, the division was renamed the School of Fine Arts. It had moved into Old North College in 1890 with the Law School, and then shifted to an old Methodist church in downtown Lawrence in 1892. Later the arts returned to Old North College. None of these buildings made for happy surroundings for the musicians and artists; Old North College showed its age; its walls cracked and its floors creaked. Nevertheless, the students and faculty persevered, forming choral groups, a student band and a faculty-student orchestra for the entertainment of the university.

In 1893, the Department of Science, Literature and the Arts converted to the College of Liberal Arts and Sciences. David H. Robinson, the other surviving member of the original faculty besides Snow, became dean. The move amounted to more than a change of name. From the push toward more elective courses in the 1880s had grown a menu of six different courses for freshmen and sophomores in the College: Modern Literature, Classical, Latin-English, General Language, General Scientific and Latin

Scientific. In 1892, that plan was tossed out; instead, freshmen took a single course with a broad curriculum aimed at exposing them to the widest variety of learning. They would encounter English literature and rhetoric, a foreign language, botany and chemistry and other fields. Sophomores had more choice among languages and sciences. Soon, upperclassmen were allowed even more freedom to choose specialized courses.

Capping those moves was a new program toward the Ph.D., approved by the regents in spring 1894. Since 1875, the university had

The student press

From the middle 1870s to 1904 various publications issued from various organizations at the university, each seeking to tell a wide audience about some slice or other of life at the University of Kansas. More or less, they were newspapers — more when they carried reports of campus doings and less when they featured long articles about narrow subjects favored by their authors. They appeared once a month or occasionally once a week, typically found financial backing from some social or special-interest group at the university and usually didn't last long. Sometimes, they simply spoiled for a fight.

At least 15 different publications popped up from 1874 to 1904, according to a count by Robert Taft in his *The Years on Mount Oread.* The first came from the Natural History Society and was called *Observer of Nature.* Its original number was dated April 1, 1874. The *Kansas Collegiate* arrived next, lasting four years until it consolidated with a monthly magazine, the *Kansas Review,* which did not disappear until 1896.

Two publications appeared once a week from the early 1880s through the early 20th century. *The University Courier* lasted from 1882 to 1895 and the *Kansas University Weekly* from 1895 to 1904.

And there were many more of shorter duration. One of those was the *University Kansan,* which had a brief life in the 1889-1890 academic year. Its name was adopted in part in 1904 by the *Semi-Weekly Kansan,* an ungainly title that was changed in 1905 to *The Kansan.* In the same year a special

Kansan Board began choosing the editor instead of the position's being filled by election. In years to come, the editor usually came from the ranks of students in the journalism courses.

In 1908, the name became *The University Kansan* and in 1912, when the newspaper achieved daily status, the *University Daily Kansan.*

The KU Band as it appeared in the 1902 Jayhawker *yearbook. Below, the first version of KU's alma mater, the "Yellow and the Blue." In the 1890s those original university colors were giving way to crimson and blue.*

offered nearly 40 master of arts degrees. The Ph.D., the highest degree granted anywhere in the United States, would require at least three years' study, an oral examination and a doctoral thesis.

In 1897, the Graduate School was established and Frank W. Blackmar named dean. The school existed to oversee the university's highest degrees, but it had no separate faculty. Its staff comprised full and associate professors on the undergraduate staffs of other schools.

In 1898, the one-year Medical School preparatory program instituted in 1879 was expanded to a two-year Medical School.

Making room

As KU became a university in reality as well as name, enrollment passed 1,000 at the turn of the century. The number of faculty doubled in the same time. Research grew, too, and as a result of all that the university once again needed more space. In 1893 KU approached the Legislature for money to build new buildings.

YELLOW AND THE BLUE.

Far above the golden valley
  Glorious to view,
Stands our noble Alma Mater
  Towering toward the blue.

CHORUS — Hail to thee our Alma Mater,
  Hail to K. S. U.
Lift the chorus ever onward,
  For the crimson hue.
      (Or) The yellow and the blue.

Far above the distant humming
  Of the busy town,
Reared against the dome of heaven,
  Looks she proudly down.

From Mount Oread's heights she gazes,
  Far beyond the Kaw;
Blessing all her sons and daughters
  Who have gone before.

Greet we then our fostering mother,
  Noble friend so true;
We will ever sing her praises —
  Dear old K. S. U.

An art class at work in 1893. Below: Each year, women dressed as men for an event called Puff Pant Prom.

They faced a different kind of Legislature, one partly controlled by the new Populist Party. The Populists had sprung up in the wake of an economic downturn that began on the plains in the late 1880s when a bubble in land prices burst. At the same time Kansas farmers faced drought, flood and bad winters. In 1893 the national economy followed suit and the first financial panic in two decades set in. Popular discontent built, and in 1893 the Populists won control of the Kansas Senate and split the vote for the Kansas House. Among the Populist causes: limits on state spending.

Snow and the regents soldiered on, anyway, asking the Legislature for an increase in the annual appropriation and for two new buildings, a library and a home for the physics program. They got no increase in the annual grant, but they did get money for new buildings.

First came the library, for which the Legislature granted money for books and equipment. It also authorized KU to use the $91,000 designated for the university in the will of

William Spooner to build the stand-alone library. Spooner was designed by Harvard-educated Henry Van Brunt, who had begun his career in Boston, where his firm designed buildings at Harvard. In 1887, Van Brunt moved his firm and later himself to Kansas City, where he created railroad stations for Union Pacific — among them the Lawrence Union Pacific depot on the north side of the Kansas River —and other buildings throughout the West. For the Spooner Library, Van Brunt employed the Romanesque style,

The first official chancellor's residence on 14th Street downhill from Spooner.

Right: The physics building, opened in 1895 and later named for Professor Lucien Blake.

originally based on early Christian churches in the south of France. The building was executed in locally quarried limestone and Dakota sandstone. On it was inscribed one of Chancellor Snow's favorite Biblical texts: "Whoso findeth wisdom findeth life."

Next to be built was the physics building. On a site southwest of University Hall rose a chateau-like stone-faced structure in a combination of Gothic and Renaissance motifs. Professor Lucien I. Blake, an expert in electricity, thermodynamics and X-rays, guided the building into being. Eventually it would be named for him. It had spacious laboratories for experiments in physics and electricity, and to reduce vibration its foundation rested on piers that reached down to bedrock. To avoid interference from magnetic fields, no iron was to be used below the third story and brass, copper and lead composed all the plumbing and fittings. Unfortunately, experiments were compromised to some extent by nails and window-sash weights. As usual, they were made of iron. The building opened in 1895.

Besides all this, the chancellor got a new house, a Victorian structure that would be built directly downhill from Spooner.

Still, KU needed more. In 1895, Snow and

The Museum of Natural History under construction.

the regents went back to the Legislature with additional construction requests. One proposed building would house the chemistry and pharmacy departments; the chemistry structure built in 1883 already was outmoded and crowded. Some chemistry students could get no time in the laboratory and pharmacy majors operated in moldy, unsanitary rooms in the basement. Another structure would serve engineering

Professor Dyche, on the way to fame as a paleontologist, and his anatomy class, alive and not so much, in the 1890s.

students for shop work, relieving the engineering classes from small rooms under the boiler house.

Also needed was a museum. In Snow Hall classrooms were crowding the collection that Snow had started and that his student, Lewis Lindsey Dyche, who was now a professor, constantly expanded. KU threw in one more request: a gymnasium.

This time, the pleas failed. In those days, the Legislature met only every other year, so KU continued on its course with the same buildings until 1897, when the regents took another run at a request. Amid continuing financial problems faced by Kansans and a wave of opposition from Populists, the legislators rejected all the new buildings and went a step farther, cutting the annual university appropriation from $100,000 to a little more than $85,000 a year. Some salaries were singled out for reduction: Snow's was cut to $4,000 from $5,000 and full professors' from $2,000 to $1,800 or less.

In early spring 1898, lightning caused a fire

A set of grotesques was carved from stone and mounted high on the outer walls of the Natural History Museum in 1903. Three would bear words. On one fanciful creature with an elephantine trunk the sculptors emblazoned "Rock Chalk." A second had "J Hawk?" A third had "KU".

that severely damaged the power plant and the existing engineering shops, shutting off electricity

A loan from Lawrence and a philanthropist's gift helped build Fowler Shops for engineering students.

and heat and forcing administrators to dismiss classes. Instead of the reluctant Legislature, the regents turned to Lawrence residents. From them they received pledges of $30,000 as a loan for a new structure. Meanwhile, Professor Blake approached a friend, Kansas City meatpacking magnate George Fowler, who was searching for something to create as a memorial to his father. Fowler gave money, eventually totaling $21,000, which, combined with the Lawrence loan, was enough to build and equip a new stone structure on the southern crest of Mount Oread. Named Fowler Shops, it opened in 1899. That same year the Legislature appropriated funds to repay the loan from Lawrence residents.

The building bore an inscription stating it had come from "the generosity of George Fowler of Liverpool, England – A gift to the young people of Kansas through his son." The elder Fowler had begun his meatpacking career in Great Britain, later expanding to New York and Chicago before opening the family plant in Kansas City in 1881.

Meanwhile, the regents honored Blake for all his work by renaming the physics building Blake Hall.

In 1899, the Legislature raised the annual appropriation and provided some of the money requested for the chemistry building. It arose northwest of Snow Hall and would be another stone-faced structure designed by J.G. Haskell, who as state architect had designed Fraser Hall. He had help from E.H.S. Bailey and other members of the chemistry faculty. An auditorium

The new chemistry building, later named Bailey Hall.

on the top floor held more than 300 students, and spacious laboratories elsewhere were equipped and ventilated well. The building opened in 1900. In 1938, after Bailey's death, the structure was named for him.

The beginning of the 20th century coincided with better times in Kansas. Populist influence receded and fiscal constraints relaxed. The 1901 Legislature granted an increased amount for operations and also $75,000 for the proposed new museum. The structure would face Spooner Library and feature an ornate design, highlighted by curious animal-like figures called grotesques, one of which bore the inscription "J Hawk" – with a question mark after the name of that most un-natural specimen.

The Museum of Natural History featured displays of North American mammals, birds and fossils, most of them collected by Dyche. In 1915, the museum would be named for him.

The non-contact sport with the round ball

Football's rise to prominence in the 1890s kept school pride buzzing through the autumn, but entire Kansas winters passed with no university sports — none, that is, until an associate professor named James Naismith joined the faculty in 1898.

Naismith, whose job was to teach physical training and to direct the chapel, had invented a game several years before for a YMCA School in Springfield, Massachusetts. He called it basketball, the object of which was to score points by tossing a ball into a basket. As devised by Naismith, the sport could be played indoors or out and also be free of the rough play of football.

Naturally, the new professor became basketball's biggest exponent on campus and he organized student and faculty teams. From watching those players, who used a court in the basement of Snow Hall, he chose a varsity team and scheduled 11 games stretching from early February to early April in 1899. Most were against YMCA teams from Kansas City, Topeka and Lawrence with games against Haskell Institute, William Jewell College and athletic clubs from Independence and Kansas City, Missouri. The team won seven games and lost four.

Naismith coached the team until 1907, when he turned it over to a former KU letterman, Forrest C. "Phog" Allen. Allen served as coach two years and then left the university. He was replaced in 1909 by W.O. Hamilton, who handled matters until Allen returned as coach in 1920. Under Hamilton, KU won five conference championships.

As it turned out, Naismith was the only KU head

James Naismith, right rear, with his first basketball team.

Forrest C. "Phog" Allen in 1920.

Megaphones at the ready, a snappily dressed squad of cheerleaders lined up at McCook Field in 1899.

KU's football team in its second year of existence, 1892.

coach to post a losing record; his teams won 55 games and lost 60.

The football team, meanwhile, had winning records most years in the early 1900s and won the Missouri Valley Conference championship in 1908. However, it had to contend with accusations of corruption that were rife in college football at the time. Indeed, KU paid certain players and kept others academically eligible despite their failing grades.

In addition, the question of the sport's brutality rose on several occasions, but were repelled by strong protests from students and alumni. Eventually, colleges around the country formed an association to create new rules aimed at making the sport at least somewhat safer.

The 1892 baseball team.

"The way…is thorny"

T he growth in buildings, courses and students was not enough for Chancellor Snow. Having seen the University of Kansas lose top professors to Ivy League schools, Snow worked to turn the tables. He began with Samuel W. Williston, whom he lured away from Yale to head the geology and paleontology programs at KU. More were to follow in the sciences and others in the humanities.

Snow's biographer, Clyde Kenneth Hyder, acknowledged in *Snow of Kansas* that devotees of the humanities suspected and occasionally complained that Snow leaned too far toward the sciences in his appointments and in what KU required of students. In Snow's defense Hyder pointed out that turn-of-the-century America was an age of vast growth in scientific inquiry. Besides, Snow proved himself an able defender of academic freedom and of teachers' individuality, so the humanities faculty stuck with him — even through salary cuts made by the 1897 Legislature.

In an era when bicycles gained great popularity, Chancellor Snow proved quite the daredevil rider.

From time to time legislators, governors and political bosses tried to influence appointments to the faculty, hoping to curry support or to pay off political debts. Also, they tried occasionally to have offending faculty members fired. In 1898, Snow complained in a letter to a regent, "If the time has come when the University cannot be administered as an educational

Carriages and crowds lined McCook Field in 1893. Spooner, Fraser and Snow Halls towered in the distance.

institution independent of political interference, I am ready to present my resignation."

Mostly, he succeeded in countering political influence. In 1897, a Populist governor tried to alter the Board of Regents so that the chancellor, at the time Snow, was no longer an ex officio member. Snow lobbied hard against the move and won that, too.

Chancellor Snow himself became a football fan. He danced on the field after one victory, hugged a student after another and defended his coach against allegations of rule-breaking by rival schools.

"Verily," he wrote an old classmate who was now himself a college president, "the way of the college builder is thorny, but there is great satisfaction in beholding a measure of success notwithstanding the many obstacles encountered."

Victors, vanquished, crimson, blue

A new game arrived at the university in the late 19th century, imported by young professors from the East and called football. In 1890, a group of students with only a captain and no coach twice played a team from Baker University and once a squad from the Kansas City YMCA, losing to the Y and splitting the games with Baker. Thus began a long tradition of the sport, and an equally long tradition of questioning the judgment of referees.

In the university team's final game against Baker, played at a field on Massachusetts Street, Professor William H. Carruth acted as the official. For the occasion, he wore a suit and bowler hat. According to *The Lawrence Journal*, as the game neared its end a KU player identified only as Coleman broke out of "a writhing, struggling mass" — the scrum-like collision of sides common in the early version of football — and scored a touchdown. KU fans, believing their side had won the game, rushed onto the field 500 strong and carried Coleman off on their shoulders. However, just before Coleman's heroic play referee Carruth had called a time out at the request of a KU player who wanted to leave the game. Carruth disallowed the Coleman touchdown, giving the victory to Baker. KU devotees refused to accept that outcome, and it would remain in dispute.

The next year, the team got a coach, English professor E.M. Hopkins, whose qualification was that he had seen the game played at Princeton. Hopkins observed well, for in an eight-game schedule in 1891 his team won seven games, tied one and lost none, including a 22-8 victory over the University of Missouri on a field in Kansas City. Among the victories were home-and-away contests with Baker and with Washburn College, with the Kansas City YMCA, and a game against Iowa in Kansas City. In the team's last game, played in Kansas City three days before Christmas, KU tied Washington University of St. Louis.

To that point, KU played its home games off campus at a field on Massachusetts Street. The university would get its own athletic field in 1892, courtesy of a man who had spoken at commencement in 1890. John James McCook, a

The Medical School

Medical education at the University of Kansas started small and stayed that way a long time. In 1879, the university began offering a one-year preparatory course that would allow students to enter two selected schools of medicine, one in Cincinnati and the other in Chicago. Students could enter the preparatory course in Lawrence having completed less than three years of high school.

Those requirements, paltry by 21st-century standards, would grow tougher but not right away. Bigger cities with more people suffering more ailments could offer more possibilities for clinical work, but two chancellors — Lippincott and Snow — resisted establishing a campus in a place other than Lawrence.

In 1894, a doctor in the Kansas City area offered land and money for a hospital in the small city of Rosedale near the state line. Still, the university resisted any move. In 1899 KU established what it called a School of Medicine, although it offered only the first two years of what typically was a four-year course.

In the early 1900s a new chancellor, Frank Strong,

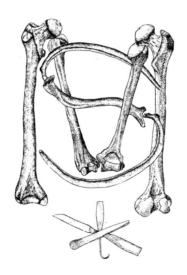

Artwork used for the Medical School section of the 1902 Jayhawker *yearbook.*

pushed the idea along. He arranged for the merger of three medical schools, two in Kansas City, Missouri, and one on the Kansas side of the metropolitan area, and by 1905 created a full, four-year course. That year, KU finally availed itself of the offer by the Kansas City physician, Simeon Bell. It built a hospital and clinical laboratory, which opened in 1907, on a Rosedale hillside that locals referred to as "Goat Hill." Students would finish the last two years of clinical work there after taking the first two years of medical classes in Lawrence.

Fortunately for the new institution, it would have excellent teachers who had graduated from some of the country's finest medical schools. They were the physician-surgeons of the Kansas City area who had been at one of the three colleges and who formed the first faculty at KU.

The school also would help improve public health with efforts to end common drinking cups, to control disease-carrying pests such as flies and rats, and to limit the spread of tuberculosis and venereal disease. Those campaigns were led by the medical dean, S.J. Crumbine, who also was secretary of the Kansas Board of Health.

New York lawyer, was also a director of the Santa Fe Railroad, and in that position had met Charles Gleed, who also sat on the KU Board of Regents. Gleed invited McCook to speak and also took him to the Senior-Faculty baseball game at the field on Massachusetts Street. McCook instantly grew fond of the university. Before returning home he turned over $1,500, to which he later added $1,000, to construct the university's own athletic field. The money went to the Athletic Board, a student-faculty group formed in 1889 to organize the school's athletic effort. McCook Field opened in fall 1892. KU played Illinois in the first football game there and won, 26-4.

Chancellor Snow himself became a football fan. He danced on the field after one victory, hugged a student after another and defended his coach against allegations of rule-breaking by rival schools.

Baseball had been played by university teams beginning in the first year of the institution's existence, but football quickly supplanted it as the dominant sport at the university. Among other things, after a typical Kansas winter the baseball season barely had time to get going before the end of spring semester. Football, on the other hand, was played in any weather and so was scheduled entirely within the academic year.

Growth of interest in football proved unstoppable, and led to the selection of new colors for the university. The early KU football teams wore red letters on their padded canvas uniforms, evidently a reaction to the occasional use at Kansas of maize and "sky blue" as colors. An early class at the university adopted those in the understanding that they were used at the University of Michigan, which had served as a model for Kansas in several ways. Debating clubs used the maize and sky blue, but football fans of the 1890s considered them too delicate for so rough a sport as football. In fact, Michigan itself, no slouch at football, altered its informally

On the day of Frank Strong's inauguration in 1902, he met with his two predecessors, Joshua Lippincott, left, and Francis Snow.

adopted "sky" or "azure" blue to a deep, dark blue.

At Kansas, then, the color would be a bold red until 1895, when complaints arose that the university was merely imitating Harvard's own color, crimson. The opinion of John James McCook was sought, and he suggested adding black or blue to crimson. In May 1896, the Athletic Board accepted the latter, and crimson and blue became KU's colors.

Change of command

In 1899, Chancellor Snow's son, who had become a newspaper reporter on assignment, fell over the side of a boat in San Francisco Bay and was lost in the choppy waters. His body was never found. The chancellor was crushed. The death, combined with the burdens of the office and health problems that his wife was already suffering, evidently caused Snow to collapse after commencement in June 1900. He spent time recovering in Colorado and Wisconsin, and then tried to return to work but could not endure the task and asked for a leave of absence. At the regents meeting on June 4, 1901, Snow turned in his resignation. He was 60.

The regents honored his years in office as "a period of marked progress," and credited "his tireless energy, his devotion to duty, his wisdom and foresight [and] his liberal and generous management of University affairs."

At the inauguration of his successor, Snow pointed to the growth of the university in his tenure. The number of students — 505 at the outset in 1891 — had more than doubled to 1,154. The faculty had increased similarly, from 34 to 79. Six new buildings had gone up, and the university had been reorganized into new schools and departments.

Frank Strong

During the proceedings, the audience applauded whenever Snow's name was mentioned. When Snow finished his remarks, they stood, cheering and waving handkerchiefs.

With that, Francis Snow stepped down, but not away from the university. He would teach a class in evolution and work on his collections, some of which by then had been moved to the Museum of Natural History. His health improved and he regained energy, enough so that he occasionally lobbied the Legislature on behalf of the university. Through the years, he continued to go on expeditions in the American West.

In 1908, while vacationing in Wisconsin, Francis Snow died of a heart ailment. His old colleagues from the 1866 faculty already were gone — Elial Rice died in 1872 and David Robinson in 1895.

A new leader and a lavish beginning

Snow's successor as chancellor, Frank Strong, came from the University of Oregon, where he had been president. The 42-year-old Strong was a native New Yorker with an undergraduate degree, a master's and a Ph.D., all from Yale. He was elected by the regents April 16, 1902, and said yes to the university and to a $1,000-a-year raise.

Despite his eastern background, Strong was familiar with the Great Plains, having spent the years 1886 to 1895 there, first in a law office in Kansas City, and then as a high school principal in St. Joseph, Missouri, and later as school superintendent in Lincoln, Nebraska. When the KU regents called, Strong had been at Oregon only three years, most of those spent unhappily battling with faculty and the Oregon regents.

Strong went to work at KU in August 1902. He was inaugurated officially in a three-day ceremony in mid-October. State officials and representatives of other colleges flocked to KU for the occasion.

On the morning of October 17, a procession of students and 300 or so alumni formed a double column from the steps of Fraser Hall to Spooner Library. Past them marched the new chancellor, the past chancellor, other administrators, regents, faculty and distinguished guests. They crossed to the new and yet unfinished museum building and stepped to a temporary platform on the first floor, where one day Professor Dyche's panorama of North and South American flora and fauna would go on display. Students, alumni and others then filed in as the Philharmonic Orchestra of Kansas City provided music. Among the dignitaries were the presidents of Yale, Cornell, Colorado, California, Missouri and Oklahoma, and the dean of arts and sciences from Harvard.

Strong was KU's first leader with no past connection to the work of clergyman, but he remained a devout Baptist. In his inaugural address, he acknowledged that a public university should not teach sectarian lessons but could follow certain Christian morals. Strong called on the university to encourage students to a "sense of moral responsibility in government…unselfish collective action for the good of the community…self-denial for the collective honor of the State."

Inauguration day ended with a dinner for more than 1,000 at the Natural History Museum. After-dinner speeches stopped after 26 when it was discovered that some of the scheduled speakers had given up and left.

Then Frank Strong — whom a Yale dean's letter of recommendation described as having "almost superhuman energy and force" — got down to work.

A constant search for support

In the years to come, that work would take Strong before the Legislature time and again, insisting on ever-larger appropriations in amounts that were astonishing by the lights of the penurious late 1890s in Kansas. In the new century, the state's economic well-being ticked up and cries for thriftiness in government dwindled. One sign of the upswing: Kansas' population from 1890 to 1900 grew by only 3 percent. From 1900 to 1910, it rose 15 percent.

As the university won many of its campaigns with state government for money, the campus filled with more new structures. To make room, KU gobbled up property along Mount Oread.

Under Strong's urging, the Alumni Association found new energy and began a publication, *The Graduate Magazine*. The idea was to keep alumni informed of the doings on Mount Oread and to make it possible for every graduate to be a spokesman for the KU cause. The university's publicity arm muscled

Uncle Jimmy and the Law School

The university began offering classes in law in fall 1878 under a part-time instructor named James W. Green, who was also a practicing lawyer and the county attorney. The first class in the Department of Law numbered 13 students, each of whom paid a $25 fee. That covered all expenses, which amounted to Green's pay.

Green's department — by 1879 he was being called "dean" — began in University Hall, moving from room to room until 1890. That year, the just-promoted School of Law took space in Old North College, a building that the university had used little since the opening of University Hall in 1872. Four years later, it returned to University Hall.

James W. Green

In 1905, the school moved into its own dedicated building, designed along the lines of a Greek temple, to the north of University Hall, now renamed Fraser. Based on a vote of the law students, the name Green Hall was recommended after the man now referred to as "Uncle Jimmy," and the regents approved. At the dedication, Green noted how the students had grown to 150 and the permanent faculty from one — himself — to four, all of them full-time.

Green proved to be a fierce defender of his school and his building. Plans to use some of the new space for liberal arts classes were scuttled after Green's students objected. Through the years, he was accused of encouraging a cult-like attitude among the law students, and of striving to build his own popularity at the expense of professors in other departments. He also minimized the need for students to have much pre-law training, not even requiring a high school diploma for admission until 1904.

A lover of football, Green served on the Athletic Board and for years held a team banquet at his home. Detractors accused him of taking it easy on football players at grading time.

"Uncle Jimmy" died in office in 1919 after 41 years as the only head of legal education. The 1920 *Jayhawker* yearbook was dedicated to him. To honor Green's service, a statue depicting him guiding a student was created by sculptor Daniel Chester French. It was placed on a tall base in front of the building that bore Green's name and unveiled in the 1920s.

Above, the Law School class of 1894. Right, the new Law School building, later named Green Hall.

up, sending out to the state's newspapers press releases containing copious information in words and images. It also made a strong push to mollify editors who had been critical of the university.

Students, meanwhile, grew worldlier and perhaps rowdier. Sports — particularly football — ratcheted up in the attention of university and public alike.

Every move, of course, went back to money, and Frank Strong proved himself the right man at the right time to get it for KU.

In 1903, Strong boldly warned that legislative cost-cutting of recent years had put the university on a downward path, not only dropping it below the universities in comparable states but also placing it on the road to doom. To stave off doom, Strong requested an appropriation of $619,000, which far more than doubled the amount provided by the state in 1901. Included in the request was a new building for the Law School and tens of thousands of dollars to finish the new Chemistry Building.

Because of a factional struggle within the dominant Republican party, KU got nothing close to what it sought. Among other items, the operating budget was cut from the $205,000

that Strong sought to $150,000. The law school building got $50,000, not the $80,000 requested. For the first time, the university was allowed to charge tuition, although it would be called "incidental fees."

Undaunted, Strong insisted that the booming Kansas economy made it the time to do "large things" for KU. From the 1905 Legislature he sought increased operating money plus funds to enlarge the campus and to build a gymnasium and a classroom structure for the growing Engineering School. This time, he was more successful, getting the gymnasium and the money for land, and the operating money he had requested. Strong's victory was incomplete, but KU celebrated nevertheless.

His effort in the next legislative session in 1907 yielded even more money, including funds to build the engineering structure and also one for mineralogy, mining and geology.

Never satisfied, Strong kept up the push, asking for appropriations stretching through the next decade for an ambitious building program. No university could sit still, he told legislators; if the University of Kansas wasn't growing, it surely was on the path to decay and death.

In 1909, for the first time, the university's annual request topped $1 million and Strong got almost all of it.

By that point in his chancellorship, the campus spread farther along Mount Oread and down its slopes. Now the main campus covered more than 163 acres, a little more than half of it purchased and most of the rest donated. As the acreage had grown, new buildings had gone up at a pace unlike anything before.

First had come a new Law School structure that allowed James Green and his students to move out of Fraser Hall; they had abandoned North College in 1894 when the physicists and electrical engineers programs moved to their new building, to be called Blake Hall. The new law building rose two stories, had a four-column portico reminiscent of a Greek temple and was ready for use by fall semester 1905. At its dedication that November, it received the name of Green Hall in honor of its longtime dean.

Next was a gymnasium west of Fowler Shops, its walls topped by castle-like crenelations. For a decade and more, indoor athletics had been conducted in basements of other buildings, first Fraser and later Snow Hall. When KU hired James Naismith in 1898, his new game, basketball, was played on a court in the basement of Snow. Those restrictive quarters caused Naismith to join Strong in petitioning the Legislature for money. The new building would be named for the late Charles Robinson, the one-time territorial governor and longtime university supporter, and

Erasmus Haworth, called "Daddy" by his students. Below, Haworth Hall, 1909.

his wife, Sara, who was still alive and who had contributed her own property to the campus. The first floor contained the gym, the second a 2,500-seat auditorium and the basement a swimming pool. Elsewhere in the building were smaller game and exercise rooms.

Robinson Gymnasium opened in May 1907 and commencement exercises took place there in June.

The campus continued its westward march. Two more buildings for the Lawrence campus were authorized and paid for by the Legislature in 1907. Construction began that year and they opened in 1909.

Three-story Haworth Hall, home for

Robinson Gymnasium, which held the university's first basketball court built for the purpose, opened in 1907.

the departments of geology and mineralogy, was named for their guiding spirit, Professor Erasmus Haworth. Haworth, called "Daddy" by his students, chaired the departments from 1892 until 1920. A prolific writer on things geological, Haworth had overseen formation of the Kansas Geological Survey in 1894. He presided over his department's move to the new hall, done in the collegiate gothic style and sitting just west of Robinson Gymnasium.

Marvin Hall, built in 1908.

West of Haworth came a larger, four-story structure for engineering. It would be named for the dean, Frank O. Marvin, who had come to KU in 1878 when his father, James Marvin, was chancellor. Of the professional schools begun in the 1890s, engineering had grown the most under its dean, who defined his students' task as "the art of directing the great sources of power in nature for the use and convenience of man."

To supply heat and power to these and other buildings, a new power plant, paid for in the same 1907 appropriation, went into operation in 1909.

Next, the university began looking to build the biggest structure to date — an administration and classroom building to accommodate constantly increasing enrollment, which had reached 2,000 by 1908, and the administrative functions to handle it. Indeed, the regents would argue that KU's administrative offices in Fraser Hall had become "absurdly inadequate, being smaller and more ill equipped than the offices of many high schools."

Grand plans were prepared for a building that would become a landmark at the center of campus.

Students crossed the campus in 1908, captured by a panoramic camera that gave a 180-degree view from Blake Hall on the left, past Fraser, Green and the Natural History Museum to Spooner on the right. In 1913, below, another panorama took in the view across Potter Lake toward Haworth, Robinson Gymnasium and Marvin.

Instead of using the state architect, the regents hired a St. Louis architect as an adjunct. Technically a member of the faculty, Montrose Pallen McArdle would receive $2,400 a year, primarily for designing the structure. He was recommended by George Kessler, the landscape architect of Kansas City's boulevards who had laid out a master plan for the KU campus with the administration building at the hub. McArdle drew up a domed structure 400 feet long with a central building, two wings and an entrance colonnade projected to cost $500,000.

As usual, the budget had to be reduced. After cutting, the central building and two wings remained but the dome, columns and much ornament disappeared. Instead of stone, yellow terra cotta faced the entire, three-story structure. Brick masonry formed the remainder of the exterior walls, which were 30 inches thick. The final style of the structure has been described by architectural historians as Classical Revival.

The new Administration Building went up

slowly, in stages determined by availability of state money. One appropriation, for $50,000, arrived in 1909; another for $75,000 arrived the next year. First to be built was the east wing, which opened in November 1911. Into it moved various departments: history, sociology, philosophy, economics, drawing and painting.

For the central portion, the state initially provided only enough money to lay a foundation. That was finished by 1913, and there the foundation sat for eight years. In 1917 came funds for the west wing. Finally, in 1921, a $250,000 appropriation arrived to construct the center of the building.

The completed, 130-room structure, still imposing even after all the cutbacks, opened in December 1923.

Schools and specialties

Buildings symbolized KU's rapid growth in the years before the World War, but programs expanded, too. The Medical School, with encouragement of land donated by Simeon Bell of Rosedale, Kansas, came into being overnight with a merger of two medical colleges then operating in Kansas City, Missouri, with a third medical college in Kansas City, Kansas.

In 1909, the regents expanded the education

department, which had been abolished in 1885 and revived as a Department of Pedagogy in the 1890s, to a full-fledged school. Although Emporia Normal had been established originally for teacher training, KU saw a distinction: it would prepare teachers for high school while Emporia focused on elementary education. The new School of Education established its own Oread Training High School to give prospective teachers practical experience.

Courses in journalism, first organized in the College of Arts in the early 1900s, were systematized in a new Department of Journalism in 1908. The department, which published *The Kansan* as a laboratory newspaper, received a full-time director in 1911. In 1912 the paper became a daily. For years, journalism classes met and *The Kansan* was produced in the old chemistry building, later called the medical building and then the journalism building. Journalism students called it "the shack."

Out with the regents

Like the University of Kansas, the Kansas State Agricultural College felt expansive in the early 1900s.

KU was proud of its decade-old College of Engineering, and rankled when the Manhattan institution added mechanical, electrical and civil engineering to its own curriculum. The Agricultural College also asked the Legislature for money to build engineering buildings. KU wanted money, too, and there would be only so much to go around. As KU leaders saw it, part of the mission of the Agricultural College always had been to teach mechanical arts —how to run machinery and use it to produce things. KU saw its engineering role as the preparation of professionals to devise that machinery, and to design and oversee the production of things, from buildings to bridges to mines and oil wells.

As KU stewed over that perceived imposition, Emporia Normal felt its own mission being compromised. There, feelings ran deep about KU's new School of Education and the university's own belief that it should train upper-level teachers, leaving training for the "common"

Left, the east wing of the Administration Building, built from 1909 to 1911 and the first part to be completed. A west wing and main hall of the building, later named Strong Hall, were not finished until 1923.

schools to Emporia. In response Emporia began its own program of training high-school teachers in various parts of the state. In 1902, the Normal School expanded its operation to a Western Branch in Hays and in 1903 to an Auxiliary Manual Training School in Pittsburg.

As these bad feelings festered, politicians in the governor's office and the Legislature tried to find ways to reduce duplication of programs of all types, among them courses offered by the university and the state colleges. Doing so would mightily please complaining constituents. In fact, various attempts to reduce overlapping among schools had been attempted since the 1870s, but none came to fruition until the new century.

The state's solution was to alter the governance of higher education in Kansas. Governor Edward Hoch brought the matter to the front in 1905, after which it was fought out in the legislatures of 1909, 1911 and 1913. Along the way, one governor vetoed a restructuring but in 1913 Governor George H. Hodges, a Democrat, signed a similar measure. Duplication among KU, Kansas State and Emporia, he complained, was out of control.

The result dismantled the half-century-old system in which each school was governed by its own Board of Regents. To replace that, the state created a Board of Administration that would oversee the work of all three institutions plus the state schools for the blind and for the deaf. The new board would contain three members, chosen by the governor and paid as full-time state employees who would serve four-year terms. On July 1, 1913, the three boards of regents went out of business, and the new Board of Administration went to work.

Among its first efforts was to consolidate business offices in Manhattan with an eye to moving them to Topeka in the future.

JAYHAWK SUFFERS ATTACK OF JINX AT DES MOINES

Although the name "Jayhawk" had been used in references to KU and its students for years, no visual representation of a Jayhawk appeared until the 20th century. The primary mascot of the football team was a bulldog kept on a leash and walked around McCook Field during games. Beginning in the early 1900s, on rare occasions a birdlike creature appeared in the yearbook to symbolize sports teams. Finally, on October 25, 1912, a distinctive and exuberant Jayhawk appeared in The University Daily Kansan, *above. Drawn by* Kansan *artist Henry Maloy, the creature represented the football team, its fans and their fortunes. Maloy, labeling his bird "Jayhawk" to make things clear to readers, used his cartoons to attribute losses, like the ones depicted at right, to a baleful creature named "Jinx."*

Occasionally, the Board of Administration took it upon itself to hire and to fire faculty without consulting the institutions' leaders. None of the state institutions of higher education was comfortable with the arrangement, not the university, or the Agricultural College or the Normal Schools, which now numbered three. In 1913 the Normal branch in Pittsburg became its own institution, as did the branch in Hays a year later.

In 1917, the scheme was changed, retaining the single Board of Administration, adding the governor as a member, and giving

Trainees, bearing wooden weapons shaped like rifles and lacking uniforms, drilled in 1917.

it control not only of the colleges and university but also of the state penitentiary, the reformatory, the state industrial schools for girls and for boys and the orphans' home.

This new version of the Board of Administration gave more power to Chancellor Strong and the heads of other institutions. In addition, because the reconstituted board had more institutions to manage, it potentially had less time to meddle in each.

Nevertheless, Strong did not care for this change in his relationship with the state. Already he had looked for work elsewhere, but nothing satisfactory turned up. Then events overseas turned the world of Americans and the American university upside down. Things would remain that way for 18 months.

Pausing to wage war

In April 1917, the United States entered the Great War in Europe on the side of France and Great Britain. At colleges across the country, male students and younger faculty became targets of recruiters and then of the military draft. Chancellor Strong, who before the U.S.

declaration of war had opposed American intervention, promptly offered the university and its resources to the war effort.

On the KU campus, college work turned to a decidedly military path. Beginning April 10, 1917, faculty members who had experience in the armed forces organized volunteers into companies for drill and exercise, giving students a military outlet. The university quickly instituted courses in mapping, telephony, explosives and military engineering. By commencement time in 1917, barely more than two months after the United States entered the war, more than 500 students had left school early for the armed services or for other work in support of the war effort, particularly on farms. That summer, Company M of the Kansas National Guard, composed mostly of university men, set up tents on the grounds of the incomplete Administration Building.

Fall enrollment in 1917 fell to 2,840, nearly 600 fewer than the year before. Daily college routine turned into something like a military training post. A whistle, substituting for a bugler blowing "Reveille," sounded at 6:30 a.m.

Workers built Student Army Training Corps barracks near Marvin Hall in 1918. They would be short-lived.

to awaken students. Classes were taught three and one-half hours in the morning and three hours in the afternoon. After that, instructors directed athletics and drills, aiming to improve the students' physical fitness for service. KU formed a University Regiment, which marched and maneuvered with little equipment and no uniforms. Those were needed at the front in Europe. Women enrolled in physical fitness, Red Cross and knitting groups.

The university's Extension Division, formed years before to take university expertise to places outside Lawrence, sent speakers around Kansas. Its employees encouraged support for the war and urged families to conserve wheat and meat needed for the troops. Chancellor Strong, a temperance advocate, and other university officials supported laws to prohibit use of food products in making alcoholic beverages.

In fall 1918 the Student Army Training Corps arrived at KU and about 500 other campuses across the country. In the SATC program, the university contracted with the federal government to train 2,500 enlisted men to become officers. Government reimbursed what

the university spent to construct barracks next to Marvin Hall and near McCook Field, and to provide faculty to teach trainees. SATC recruits — who also received army uniforms, equipment, food, tuition and fees — were to study a wide range of subjects ranging from regular collegiate courses to some courses altered for military use. The military required the quarter system for SATC, so the university converted from its semester schedule.

The men were sworn in October 1, 1918, in a ceremony at McCook field. *The University Daily Kansan* complimented the event as "without pomp" and intended for one purpose: "that the Hun may be more thoroughly and expeditiously licked."

However, despite considerable upheaval to prepare for SATC, the program accomplished little. Within days of the swearing-in, the influenza pandemic that had spread through Europe, South America and the United States reached Lawrence. It affected mainly young people, particularly those living in dormitories and barracks, and so it found plenty of targets on campuses and in places such as the new SATC

barracks.

On October 8 the university closed, SATC and all, to try to halt the spread of the disease. Students were told not to leave Lawrence lest other cities be infected, nor to gather in large groups. Temporary infirmaries were set up and medical students, faculty members and townspeople worked to treat the ailing. Ten of the SATC students and 22 other KU students died of influenza, and at one point more than 700 students were afflicted by it. Classes reopened November 8, and three days later the armistice ended the Great War. The next month, the Student Army Training Corps program shut down and the barracks built only months before at McCook Field and Marvin Hall were dismantled.

Peacetime returns

Amid the victory celebrations after the war, sentiment rose to establish a Reserve Officer Training Corps on campus. By early 1919 it was approved by more than 1,000 students, the Faculty Senate and the Board of Administration. That fall, however, it was only with difficulty that the university persuaded more than the minimum of 100 men to apply. Evidently, the experience

with SATC failed at first to generate much carry-over enthusiasm.

Total university enrollment, on the other hand, surpassed 3,200, straining Lawrence's capacity to house all the students. The increase in students was accompanied by an increase in automobiles on campus, and for the first time parking became a problem.

Strong, meanwhile, decided that he had spent enough of his legendary energy managing a university. The loss of student lives in military service and in the flu epidemic affected him deeply, causing "personal shock from which I found it very difficult to recover."

Despite his hard work and excellent results on behalf of the university, Strong had never been able to connect with students and alumni the way his predecessor, Francis Snow, had. His critics often made it hard on him. Strong had pushed the university extension effort in an attempt to win support from around the state, but his foes argued that the effort only taxed the university's abilities to fulfill its basic mission — teaching students. Some alumni protested Strong's opposition to staging the KU-Missouri football game in Kansas City. Strong believed the spectacle drew too much gambling, drinking and general rowdiness and thought things would be better controlled if the game were held on the two campuses.

In September 1919, at age 60, Strong announced that he would resign effective June 1920. He would teach in the KU Law School until 1933, when he suffered a heart attack that led to his death a year later, one day after he turned 75 years old. To honor his years of work, the university named its Administration Building after him — Frank Strong Hall.

"The great changes that have come over the world in the last five years," Strong wrote in 1919, "require many new adjustments."

That was prophetic. The 1920s would rattle the foundations of society, and of college life.

WILLIAM T. FITZSIMMONS

BORN at Burlington, Kansas, April 18, 1889. Attended St. Aloysius Parochial School and St. Mary's College. Graduated from Kansas University in 1910, and received his M. D. in 1912. Studied further in New York and England. Commissioned lieutenant in Medical Reserve Corps, and was killed in an air raid on his hospital in France, September 17, 1917.

The FIRST Kansas University man killed in the GREAT WAR.

High Times, Hard Times

Americans put the Great War behind them only with difficulty. The intensity of the conflict, its distance from home and the advent of new and terrible weapons made the losses of young life saddening for everyone.

The 1919 *Jayhawker* yearbook opened with 27 pages of testimonials to individual students, former students and alumni of the university killed in combat. Many died in ways previously unknown in warfare. Among the first three named in the yearbook, one died in an air raid and two died in poison gas attacks. Still more lost their lives fighting at Belleau Wood, St. Mihiel, the Marne and the Argonne Forest. The yearbook's effort — its pages were labeled "The Peace Edition" — signaled only the beginning of remembrance at the University of Kansas.

In fall 1920 alumni, faculty and students kicked off a movement to raise money to create memorials to those who served and those who died. It was named the "Million Dollar Drive." Sorting through various proposals for memorials,

Facing page: The first KU alumnus and the first U.S. medical officer killed in the World War.

the leaders of the drive settled on a Victory Stadium and a Loyal Service Building or University Service Building. The former would become Memorial Stadium and the latter the Kansas Memorial Union.

They were part of one of the greatest building booms in the history of the university, which raced through the 1920s alongside fast dancing, jazz music, changing fashion and diminishing formality.

The Decade that Roared

"The tendency in all affairs now is to cut extravagance and strive for more simplicity," the 1920 KU yearbook stated. Indeed, after World War I America experienced a brief economic slowdown, but soon it was reversed by good times. The yearbook's sentiment for simplicity would prove short-lived, as did the long skirts worn by female students and the caps worn by male students in the first years of the decade.

As the 1920s unfolded, the campus became awash in parties and dances for students, whose number surpassed 4,000 by 1925. There were the Hallowe'en party, the Follies and the May

Dancers gathered on the basketball court at Robinson Gymnasium in 1924 . Below: Two dressed for Hobo Day in 1923.

Fete. Various KU organizations sponsored the Freshman Frolic, Soph Hop, Junior Prom and Senior Cake Walk. Also on the schedule: the Billboard Ball, Hobnail Hop, Law Scrim and Journalism Jazz. Weekends featured all-campus Varsity Dances. Big-name bands came to KU to play.

Even as hemlines rose among women and caps and hats disappeared from men's heads, students occasionally descended into complete informality, as they did on Hobo Day. Invented in 1923 as part of homecoming festivities, Hobo Day called for students to wear raggedy clothes, smudge their faces with burnt cork and in general to appear

outlandishly destitute. Like homecoming itself, the idea was to celebrate the university by cheering for football.

Sports and all their accompaniments — pep rallies, cheerleaders, band music, banquets, pennants and mascots — grew into a fixture of American college life in the 1920s, and KU joined the frenzy. Football was such an attraction that by spring 1921 more than half a million dollars had been pledged to the Million Dollar Drive. That was enough to start work on the top priority, the new memorial football stadium.

Exuberant over the success of the fund drive, the university on May 10, 1921, threw a special

Gone in a day: The bleachers at McCook field were dismantled and the lumber carried away by volunteer students and faculty.

Stadium Day. Classes were called off and students asked to present themselves at McCook Field to help tear down the old wooden bleachers. Hundreds of students and scores of faculty made short work of the structure. After lunch and speeches, the time came to break ground for the new stadium.

The honor went to a slender, white-haired man dressed in work clothes who skillfully guided a horse-drawn plow across the old field. He made an impressively straight furrow, but he was not a farmer brought in for the occasion. The plowman was the new chancellor of the University of Kansas, Ernest H. Lindley.

Amiable and open

Less than one year before, on June 8, 1920, Lindley had been picked for the job by the Board of Administration. He was 50 years old

Ernest H. Lindley

and previously president of the University of Idaho. Lindley had received his undergraduate and master's degrees from Indiana University and a Ph.D. from Clark University in Massachusetts. He also had studied in Europe and at Harvard. Lindley's specialties were philosophy and psychology, and his doctoral dissertation explored the relation of puzzle-solving to learning.

Like Frank Strong, Lindley stood tall and moved with energy. But where Strong acted reserved and formal, Lindley proved polite, open and amiable. He got along well with students and faculty and worked hard to appeal to alumni. He sought out their ideas and asked them to support the university with their legislators and their money, and they responded. It was not out of character for Ernest Lindley to put his shoulder to the plow on behalf of KU.

Early in Lindley's tenure, the Alumni Association was reinvigorated. First under Alfred G. Hill from 1920 to 1924, and then Fred Ellsworth, who would serve almost 40 years as its leader, the association vigorously increased its effort to make alumni feel a continuing part of the university. It succeeded; membership rose from 1,500 in 1919 to 3,500 in 1929.

The Kansas University Endowment Association, which was created in 1891 to receive any gifts that came KU's way, had accumulated only a few hundred dollars in its first 30 years. When the retiring dean of the College of Liberal Arts and Sciences, Olin Templin, became secretary of the Endowment Association, he persuaded Lindley to help create a board of

Watkins and Miller halls, among the gifts of Elizabeth Watkins.

trustees. The board would oversee a systematic effort to bring in donations.

Among the donors the new board rounded up was Solon Summerfield, an 1899 KU graduate who made a fortune producing silk hosiery and now endowed a set of scholarships. Elizabeth Watkins, widow of Lawrence millionaire Jabez Wakins, gave more than $2 million to the university, contributing to a scholarship dormitory, Watkins Hall, just north of her home. It opened in 1925. She would also contribute to a second scholarship dorm, Miller Hall, which opened 12 years later. Both halls were for women. Eventually, her estate would give the university a new chancellor's home.

Success in business had led to the accumulation of fortunes by Summerfield and Watkins, and business was the engine of the 1920s. Early in his chancellorship, Lindley moved to make business study a prominent part of KU's offerings by establishing a School of Business.

"Commerce," he said, "has become a learned profession." Industrial production and organization, he believed, engaged a large part of the creative intelligence of the age.

Finally overcoming objections from his Department of Economics, Lindley in 1924 saw the creation of a two-year School of Business. Its dean would be a Johns Hopkins Ph.D., Frank Stockton, whose choice pleased the previously reluctant economics faculty.

Despite the money being made in America at the time, and despite all Lindley's new efforts at outreach, the Million Dollar Drive after its quick start slowed down. Payments ran behind pledges, and the newly created University of Kansas Memorial Corporation at first could come up with only about $290,000 cash for the stadium. It was decided, then, to build the structure in phases. First would come part of the stands on the east and the west sides of the football field. When enough money arrived, plans called for the stadium to form a "U."

Thanksgiving Day 1921 overlooking the new stadium. On the field, KU beat Missouri, 15-9.

The tough 1923 football team did not allow a touchdown and lost no games, but played to three ties.

Construction began on the scaled-down version July 16, 1921. Despite the fact that the still-incomplete stands could seat only 5,000 spectators, on October 29 the Jayhawks played their first game on their new field, beating Kansas State, 21-7. By the time the Missouri football team came to town for a Thanksgiving Day game that year, the first phase was complete. More than 15,000 watched KU beat the Tigers, 15-9. The stadium was dedicated formally on Armistice Day, November 11, 1922.

KU lost that day to Nebraska, 28-0. But the football squad had demonstrated time and again that it could overcome loss. Indeed, up to the time that Memorial Stadium arose, KU showed every promise of becoming a consistent football power in the midlands.

The rise of sports

In the three decades since the university fielded its first football team in 1890, KU won two of every three games it played, and suffered only five losing seasons. From time to time the team enjoyed spectacular success. Twice it won 10 games, twice it went undefeated and untied and in 1908 the team won its conference championship.

The mustachioed inventor of basketball with the 1923 team and his premier pupil, Phog Allen. Adolph Rupp, later coach at Kentucky, stood in the back row at left. Right: James Naismith with female players in 1922.

Based on that performance, and with the prospect of playing in a big new stadium, there was every reason to hope that football would continue at an above-average pace.

Reality turned out otherwise. In the 1920s, the football program fell into a pattern that would continue for decades: grand but rare successes followed by season after season of mediocrity. The 1923 team allowed not a single touchdown, but tied three of its games and finished only in third place in the Missouri Valley conference. From 1920 to 1929 KU came in no higher than that, and most years in fifth place or worse. Coaches

came and went. Among them, Potsy Clark lasted five years; his teams won 16 games, lost 17 and tied six.

In 1930, the team, coached by Bill Hargiss, won the championship of the new Big Six conference, but fell back to 1920s-like records through the rest of that decade.

It was small wonder that in the 1920s football, by then clearly the collegiate spectator sport nationwide, met stiff competition for the attention of KU students, faculty and alumni.

Fashion, as depicted in 1921, would change as the decade wore on. So would the look of the union when it was built.

Preceding pages: The university from the air, 1923.

Most years, Forrest C. "Phog" Allen and his basketball teams gave the university much more to cheer for.

Allen had played for James Naismith in 1906-1907 and coached the next two years, the team's first playing in the new Robinson Gymnasium. He had departed to study osteopathy and then to coach at Warrensburg Teacher's college in Missouri. In his absence, KU enjoyed success on the court. Allen returned as athletic director and coach in the 1919-1920 academic year, and from the 1921-22 season through the next five, KU lost no more than three games a year. The team won the hearts of people on campus, in Lawrence, and throughout the state.

In the 1920s the basketball team won five conference titles outright and tied for one. It would win or tie for seven more in the 1930s. All came under Allen.

Activity atop The Hill

The other memorial to those who fought in the World War, a student union, had to wait until yet more money could be raised. Finally, in 1924 planners chose a site north of the Natural History Museum and in 1925 work began on the union.

By fall semester 1927, construction was far enough along that a cafeteria area called the Commons opened for service. Two months later, visitors to the union could also occupy the main-floor lounge. As more money came in, more sections were opened but progress was slow. Not until 1934 would workers finish the ballroom; completion of the Kansas Room took until 1939.

Meanwhile, other buildings not dependent on contributions arose along Mount Oread. The Legislature in the early 1920s showed a generous spirit, and the year 1923 proved particularly active. That year construction began on a new library. Spooner Library had been more than

The Kansas Union in the 1920s, above, and the new Watson Library, below.

adequate for the needs of 1894 and remained in good physical condition, but by the 1920s the university's book collection exceeded Spooner's space by at least half. A new library, placed south of Snow Hall and west of Fraser and designed in collegiate gothic style, opened in September 1924. It was named for Carrie Watson and could hold 800 students. Even this new library's capacity would soon be strained by its growing book collection.

Within years, Spooner would be converted into an art museum, housing first the art

In 1930, new Snow Hall was open..

collection of a Kansas Citian, Mrs. W.B. Thayer. It was renamed Spooner-Thayer Art Museum.

Also in 1923 the university opened its first large dormitory. It was the inspiration of Alberta L. Corbin, the adviser for women. Corbin had complained to the administration that female students and freshmen women in particular had to rent private rooms that were far from campus, often uncomfortable and too expensive — not to mention unsupervised. She successfully lobbied the Legislature for money for a new hall housing 128 women. Built on the site of Old North College, which had been demolished by 1919, it was named Corbin Hall.

In addition, December 1923 marked the opening of the central and last portion of the Administration Building, which had gone up in stages since 1911. With that, administration offices moved out of their old, cramped spaces in Fraser and into the yellow

The rakish campus humor magazine Sour Owl *poked fun at politics, football foes and prudery. At left, a well-fed Herbert Hoover and a starving Santa led off one Depression issue. The* Owl *lasted until the 1950s.*

terra-cotta building where they remained into the 21st century.

As 19th century buildings aged, the need arose for even more new ones. A 1923 faculty report declared that Snow Hall was failing structurally — some inhabitants swore they felt it quiver on windy days — had become a firetrap and was infested with vermin. The complaints about Snow extended as far back as 1916, when experts learned that the foundation was inadequate and the overall construction poor. In the late 1920s, with a $200,000 grant from the state, KU built a new and larger Snow Hall dedicated to the sciences and, as before, to the one-time chancellor and professor who championed them, Francis H. Snow. The building went up west of the Administration Building

Cheering at a crowded 1935 basketball game at Hoch Auditorium. Below: Hoch from the outside.

beginning in 1928 and classes began there in January 1930. At its dedication, a former student of Snow's who was by that point a professor himself intoned, "The spirit of its founder lives on in the new Snow Hall."

Across the street from Snow stood another recently constructed building, this one intended to hold the increasing number of concerts, lectures, convocations and other events on campus. The new building, paid for by $350,000 in grants from the Legislature and designed in the collegiate gothic style, was named for a former governor and member of the Board of Administration, E.W. Hoch.

It would also become home court for the varsity basketball team, having been planned with the game in mind. The main floor and two balconies of the auditorium faced the stage, but permanent seating occupied only the rear part of the main floor. The front section, nearest the stage, was covered in hardwood and contained enough space to hold a basketball court. For

concerts, temporary seating was placed on it. When the basketball Jayhawks played, the seating was removed. The new building provided room for about 3,500 spectators for basketball. That easily outdistanced the small numbers packed to the rafters at Robinson Gymnasium, where the team had played for two decades.

The university dedicated Hoch in fall 1927 and on January 6, 1928, Phog Allen's Jayhawk

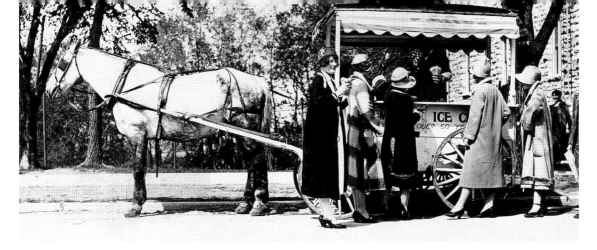

Campus sights of the 1920s: An ice cream cart and, below, any old place to park for those not riding the streetcar.

basketball team played its first game there, beating Washington University, 29-26.

Months before, the football stadium finally took the U-shaped form that had been planned all along, bringing its capacity to 38,000. The Million Dollar Drive had never reached its goal, so to complete the job the Athletic Board chartered a Physical Education Corporation, which issued $350,000 in bonds to be paid by sales of tickets to games.

The university's other campus expanded, too. In 1920, the city of Rosedale along with alumni and friends of KU bought for the School of Medicine 15 acres of level ground south of the original "Goat Hill" site, which had proved largely inaccessible. With $435,000 granted by the 1921 Legislature, the university built a new Bell Memorial Hospital, which opened in 1924. A Nurses' Home and another structure were built with $300,000 granted by the 1927 Legislature. By then, Rosedale had been absorbed by Kansas City, Kansas.

Fired and reinstated, and the regents return

As a time of remarkable growth for the university, the 1920s might have given Chancellor Lindley great satisfaction. However, success in fundraising and alumni support did not bring equal success in the realm of getting along with politicians. Within a few years, relations between the university and the state, and in particular between the chancellor and the governor, strained beyond the breaking point.

Problems began with the Board of Administration, which had managed Kansas' university and colleges since 1913, when separate boards of regents were abolished. The intent at the time was to coordinate leadership of the institutions, reduce or eliminate duplicated efforts and thus save money.

Along the way, some unlikely bedfellows

Alpha Phi Alpha fraternity in 1923.

In 1926, students could bathe in the waters of Potter Lake with the Administration Building as backdrop.

were added to the board's higher education portfolio. In 1917 the Board of Administration also took under its wing the state penitentiary, the reformatory, the industrial schools, the orphans' home and the state fish hatchery. The number of agencies and branches it supervised, which grew to 27, proved too large to effectively administer. Vast as the board's span of control was, its duties as set by the Legislature remained murky.

Governor Jonathan Davis

Not surprisingly, Chancellor Lindley and the heads of the other schools of higher learning in Kansas chafed at being part of this menagerie of state institutions, and they asked for a study of the board's effectiveness. A three-member committee of the U.S. Bureau of Education was commissioned to investigate. It reported that KU and the colleges ought to have their own, separate oversight body, one that set broad policy and let institutions' administrators figure how

to implement it. The proposed body should contain nine members who would be prominent Kansans serving without pay, named by, but not including, the governor,

Far from bowing to the suggestions of that report, the Board of Administration tightened the screws. In 1923 board members newly appointed by Governor Jonathan Davis, a Democrat who campaigned on an austerity platform, concluded among other things that KU had too many deans. To back up the point, the four-member board — which included the governor as an ex officio member — turned down Lindley's requests to raise the deans' pay. Going beyond that, the board pushed the university and other institutions to open some campus jobs to patronage. It strongly suggested that KU hire its buildings and grounds workers based on their loyalty to the Democratic Party. When KU's buildings and grounds

Facing page: Jayhawk Boulevard, as depicted in the 1929 yearbook.

In 1926, Chancellor Lindley stood at the center of a group dedicating the "Uncle Jimmy" Green statue.

superintendent balked, the board removed him — over Chancellor Lindley's strong objection. About the same time, Republicans began blasting both the board and the Democratic governor for their handling of matters at the KU Medical School.

At the time, Kansas governors served two-year terms, meaning that Davis came up for re-election in November 1924. He lost by a landslide, but despite his lame-duck status he launched a final assault on Lindley. One complaint stemmed from the handling of an incident in which four KU students were suspended after being accused of drunken driving. Another concerned the university's purchasing and spending procedures.

In response to Davis' charges, Lindley met with the Board of Administration and the result was contentious. On December 27, the Democrat-dominated body fired Lindley. The lone Republican on the board disagreed. Davis, only weeks away from leaving the governor's office, announced Lindley's dismissal, calling it justified because the chancellor had proven incompetent,

insubordinate, aloof and slow to act on directives from the board.

Lindley hired lawyers to fight the ouster but in early January his challenges failed in court. He won, however, in the court of public opinion. KU alumni organized a telegram campaign aimed at the incoming Republican governor, Ben Paulen, who was to be sworn in within days. Newspapers backed Lindley, as did other educators.

Shortly after the new governor entered office, he met with the Board of Administration. It promptly rescinded its order and reinstated Lindley to the chancellorship.

That did not end matters. Urged on by Lindley and other university supporters, Governor Paulen pushed through the 1925 Legislature a measure removing the university and the state colleges from the Board of Administration. The new law created a nine-member Board of Regents to govern only the five institutions of higher learning. Its members would be appointed by the governor, but the governor would not be a member.

A turn for the worse

Restored to office, Lindley returned to leading the university through its growth in the booming 1920s. In fall 1929 enrollment reached 4,079 at the Lawrence campus and 170 at the Medical Center, totaling 4,249 — the largest ever. When that academic year began, the country rolled along amid good times for employment and industry. They would be the last for a while.

Not long into fall semester 1929, the stock markets crashed. Credit tightened, industries cut back, and jobs were lost. By the end of the 1929-1930 academic year, economic matters looked as grim as they had in the early 1890s. They would become even grimmer.

The U.S. economy fell into what became known as the Great Depression. Like the stock market and the banking system, KU enrollment began to decline, although not as far as the markets. On the Lawrence campus fall enrollment had topped 4,000 for the first time in 1925 and through the rest of that decade it hovered around that number. In 1931, however, only 3,886 showed up for fall classes at Lawrence. In 1933, enrollment bottomed out at 3,459.

The problems that affected the entire country were compounded in the Central Plains. On the farm, which still represented a major part of the Kansas economy, drought took over in 1932 and settled in. For hundreds of miles to the west of Lawrence, high winds blew over dry fields, creating dust storms. The storms struck eastern Kansas, too. On March 20, 1935, drivers on the KU campus turned on their headlights in mid-afternoon. Through those same summers of the middle 1930s, in the days when air conditioned offices and homes were mostly unheard of,

On March 20, 1935, drivers on the KU campus turned on their headlights in mid-afternoon.

temperatures topped 100 degrees for days on end.

Reflecting the decline in farm and other incomes in Kansas, and thus in state revenues, the Legislature in 1931 trimmed the university's grant by $56,000 from the amount authorized in 1929. The 1933 Legislature cut nearly three-quarters of a million dollars from the 1931 amount. Faculty and administration salaries were chopped and KU instituted cost-cutting measures; one of them encouraged the use of penny postcards instead of letters with three-cent stamps.

The savings were not enough. The 1935 Legislature trimmed the KU appropriation to a point barely above $2 million. That was more than $810,000 below the authorization of 1929. Only in 1937 did the appropriation begin to rise, and it did again in 1939. Nevertheless, the 1939 total still fell below what had been granted a decade earlier.

Instead of a steady diet of growth in people and buildings, the university had to concentrate on maintaining what it already had, and to minimize losses. As did the rest of the country, KU turned to survival instead of bold initiatives.

A harder life, but still some fun

For students, the Depression cut deeply into money for the necessities of college life — room and board, books and tuition. The decline in enrollment provided one sign of that.

For students who had to work their way through school, anyway, the decline in jobs hit hardest. In January 1934, with urging from Chancellor Lindley, the federal government made available money for part-time jobs to up to 350 students. Their pay was $15 a month. Recipients worked as research assistants, clerks and stenographers in various departments, including Watson Library and the hospital in Kansas City, Kansas. The program began as the College Student Employment Project and continued in 1935 as the National Youth Administration.

Hard times greatly reduced cash available to students for luxuries, such as fancy clothes and

An affectionate couple of Jayhawks marked the 1935 yearbook.

cars and flashy entertainment. Entertainment survived, though reduced in scope. In 1930, student managers continued to stage dances: the Hope, the Frolic, the Prom and the Senior Cake Walk lived on. So did the weekly Varsity dances, proceeds from which aided various projects of the Men's Student Council and the Women's Self Governing Association. Three student dance bands typically provided the music, because professional bands had become prohibitively expensive.

The 1934 *Jayhawker* yearbook claimed that, "as far as the spirit of fun and frivolity is concerned, there is no depression apparent on the Hill. There are no flags at half-mast for the youth of the campus."

That same year the yearbook itself, whether for financial reasons or reasons of convenience, went from a single volume that was printed in late spring to a multi-part "magazine" book, printed in segments through the school year. Students who ordered what was now called the *Jayhawker* magazine annual received a three-peg binder to house the entire school year's publications.

"At the end of the year you will have the largest, finest JAYHAWKER that has ever been published," the editors announced. "It will look exactly like a book. IT WILL BE A BOOK."

Toward the end of the 1930s hard times began to soften, if only a bit. On the Lawrence campus, enrollment squeezed back above 4,000 in 1935 and wavered above that mark the rest of the decade. The story was different for the School of Medicine, where the number of students rose almost every year through the decade of the Depression, from 189 in 1930 to 268 in 1939.

The campus in Kansas City, Kansas, saw most of the new publicly funded construction, too. After 1937, a combination of money from the state and federal governments, from the proceeds of the hospital and from private gifts led to the building of a children's pavilion, a clinic building, a laboratory for research and others.

In Lawrence, Elizabeth Watkins continued to give money that enabled construction of new scholarship halls. Already she had provided a new student hospital. When she died in 1939, Watkins' home was left to the university as a new residence for chancellors.

Changing of the guard

Throughout Lindley's tenure had come outbursts of political hubbub, and his battle with the Board of Administration was only one of them. In the early 1920s, a professor of zoology came under attack from an angry Topekan for teaching the idea of biological evolution. Economics professor John Ise, meanwhile,

Watkins Hospital in 1931.

enjoyed telling his classes how President Calvin Coolidge served as "a tool in the hand of the big business interests." He also wrote a book calling for nationalizing the U.S. petroleum industry. Neither position was much admired by pro-Republican Kansas businessmen, particularly oilmen. On campus appeared a publication called *The Dove*, which had as its platform peace, opposition to the military and to religion, too.

Late in the 1930s, the Kansas House of Representatives instituted an investigation into the university's influence on a Dodge City student, Don Henry, who entered college a religious and by all accounts patriotic young man, but became interested at KU in the Young Communist League and wound up fighting and dying in Spain's Civil War. The House probe was derailed, but the regents conducted their own, finding that Henry had been influenced leftward while a student, but not by any faculty or other officials of the university.

In 1938, Lindley grew so concerned about the university's image in Kansas that he appointed a committee to study what could be done. The committee, according to Clifford Griffin, told a

Lindley and his successor, Deane Malott, in 1939.

the Depression, when the state severely reduced its appropriations, leading to substantial cuts in salaries. Lindley's tenure, as it happened, would end on the doorstep of a second World War.

He would take a leave of absence, after which he expected to come back to teach at KU. However, in the middle of a round-the-world trip, he became sick in China. Ernest Lindley died aboard a ship in the Pacific Ocean on August 21, 1940 and was buried at sea.

An alumnus takes over

As Lindley's successor, the regents turned to Deane W. Malott, a 1921 graduate of KU who had gone on to teach at Harvard and to serve as assistant dean of its Graduate School of Business Administration. Malott was born in Abilene and received his undergraduate degree from KU in economics and journalism. He was the first person born in Kansas and the first graduate of KU to become chancellor. After KU, Malott got a master's in business administration from Harvard, spent several years in the business world and wrote several books.

The regents offered him the job April 10, 1939 and he began work that fall. That semester enrollment reached 4,369 on the Lawrence campus and 268 at the medical school.

Unlike the multi-day celebration that marked the inauguration of Frank Strong in 1902, the 41-year-old Malott made his ceremonial inauguration a simple one: A single convocation of the university at which he made a speech.

In it, he proposed no great changes, but within a year acknowledged what was going to define his own role:

"I have a feeling that public relations is one of my biggest jobs," he wrote. "We must constantly be at work to get the University off this Hill and out over the state. There is a good deal going on and we need to have all of this interpreted to the people of the state."

As part of the university's wish list for

sad tale of opportunities missed. It suggested that the chancellor pay better attention to the Legislature and also bemoaned *The University Daily Kansan* — read by editors throughout the state — as sensationalist and gossipy. Across the board, KU should do better; departments could promote themselves to the public, the Extension Division ought to be enlarged, more positive news ought to issue from the university News Bureau.

Perhaps it was no wonder that Lindley, whose tenure would be the longest of any of KU's chancellors into the next century, decided to step down. On December 1, 1938, he resigned effective in June 1939. That would fall about four months before the date he was to turn 70, the university's retirement age. Lindley's time in office was marked by transition from the aftermath of a World War, through heady days of building and growth in infrastructure, budget and enrollment. He also presided over dismal economic times in the 1941 Legislature, Malott pushed for more buildings. First should come a structure to house research and teaching in mineral resources. Petroleum production and mining, he pointed out, ranked behind only agriculture in the Kansas economy. He also asked to expand Watson Library, which now contained 200,000 more books than its stated capacity, a building for fine arts and new space for the schools of education and business. Malott recommended a new laboratory and other buildings at the Medical School in Kansas City, Kansas.

He even recommended that once-proud Fraser Hall, its walls unsteadier than ever, be demolished and replaced.

The Legislature gave KU most of what it asked in dollars, including $400,000 for the new mineral resources building. It also instituted a property tax for buildings at the state-controlled schools, aiming to provide a regular fund through which long-term plans could be made. Additionally, the Legislature enabled the state institutions of higher education to pass some of the costs of dormitories and student unions on to students through fees.

With the legislative battles won, the university turned to celebrating the 75th anniversary, or Diamond Jubilee.

The five-day event in early June was highlighted by the presence of students from every year of KU history, dating back to one person who attended in 1866. To give the campus an antiquarian feel, hitching posts were installed in various spots and streetlights were decorated to look like gas lamps.

As a child growing up in Elkhart, Kansas, Glenn Cunningham's legs were severely burned. He overcame the injury to become one of the greatest milers of the 1930s, winning an NCAA championship for KU.

War and Peace, Bigger and Better

As the 1940s began, America slowly clawed its way out of the Great Depression. A generation accustomed to scarcity, however, remained cautious about the future and about spending, particularly on a college education. The evidence was clear at the University of Kansas, where in 1941 fall semester enrollment barely topped 4,000 — several hundred fewer than any other fall in the previous seven years.

Within five years, that trend would change radically, and many of the youth who had been numbed by financial constraints would flood KU and other American campuses. The difference was World War II, a grueling three-plus years that cost more than 400,000 American lives but also put the U.S. economy back on its feet. Among the hundreds of thousands of service members who survived the conflict, many thousands returned to finish college or embark on a delayed degree.

Aided by the GI Bill, veterans swarmed into classrooms and brought an unprecedented maturity to student life. They would graduate to help form the largest and best-off middle class in American history. And they made babies in

Facing page: Navy trainees marched in 1942.

Cover illustration of the fall issue 1942 Jayhawker

unprecedented numbers, a boom that within two decades would form the biggest generation of students so far, one that would leave other unforgettable marks on KU and other campuses.

War or no? The debate ends

Three months after the beginning of fall semester 1941, on December 7, Japanese forces attacked the U.S. Naval Base at Pearl Harbor, Hawaii. The suddenness of the event stunned everyone concerned with the university and with the United States. Right away the new state of the world announced itself with news of two KU war dead: On December 7 at Pearl Harbor, Eddie Olson of the class of 1937, and on December 8 in the Philippines, a former student, Max Louk.

The prospect, even the inevitability, of war had been on the minds of students and administrators, but no one knew how it might begin until December 7.

In the weeks beforehand, a few anti-war editorials had appeared in *The Kansan*, counseling against America's intervening in the conflict already raging in Europe and Asia. An unsigned editorial in the *Jayhawker*'s first quarterly issue of fall 1941 cautioned readers against unquestioning

Navy machinists trained in the shops at Fowler Hall. To train officers, the V-5 and later V-12 programs began.

devotion to America's "definite path toward war."

"We are still divided as to whether England's fight is our fight, whether Russia's fight is our fight," the writer pronounced. "Brave people of America, you have proved your ability to fight courageously, but you have never proved your ability to think correctly. If you have resigned yourself to the decision of others, you are not worthy of being a free people."

A few pages farther on, the fall 1941 *Jayhawker* featured facing essays, one in favor of intervention, the other opposed.

But in the aftermath of Pearl Harbor, the third issue of the same yearbook made it clear how the world — and attitudes toward war — had changed. On the cover was a young man examining a message from the Selective Service. Because a U.S. territory had been attacked, the yearbook editors and students and faculty generally fell in with the war effort.

The university altered its schedule. Easter break was eliminated and the summer session extended so that students who stayed enrolled throughout the year could get their degrees in two and one-half years. In 1943, KU again changed its schedule, this time to a trimester format of 16-

"Beginning classes for the day were set at 7:30. Many a morning...I hurriedly and doggedly made the bus to the Hill in a darkness so black that it but added to the unreality of the situation. The bus reached the campus in time for its passengers to come to attention as the bugle sounded its call for the raising of the flag in front of Strong Hall.

"Mount Oread was thus an armed camp, and the rhythmic tramp of soliders and sailors going and coming to class or at drill was the most characteristic sound of the day....On October 1 (1943), there were some 4,000 students on the Hill....Half of these were in uniform, the remaining half civilians. Of the civilian half, less than 400 were men; women thus outnumbering the civilian men better than three to one."

— *Chemistry Professor Robert Taft,*
in his The Years on Mount Oread.

week terms, which lasted the rest of the war.

Even wartime spirit gave way at one point, however, when students and parents rebelled against reductions in Christmas holiday vacation. In order to make room for a trimester in mid-1943, the university reduced Christmas break to four days. In protest, a crowd of students gathered in front of the chancellor's office in Strong Hall. Things remained peaceful. The next Monday the administration re-considered and expanded the break to nine days.

Requirements were altered, too. Physical fitness courses became mandatory, along with lectures on the causes of the war. Nationwide

rationing to save key materials for the war effort led to shortages of tires and gasoline, and the number of automobiles on the road dwindled.

"The University of Kansas has given distinguished service to our nation" in other wars, Chancellor Deane Malott told *The Graduate Magazine*. "It will do so again."

Sailor uniforms appeared on campus. The Navy in July 1942 instituted its V-12 program, which trained prospective officers and filled classrooms depleted by the draft and enlistments. Eligible were high school seniors, enlisted men and students enrolled in the Navy college reserve program. Five hundred V-12 students

Dancing at the Dine-A-Mite on 23rd Streeet. Facing page: Flags of the world hung at Strong Hall's entry.

soon arrived. Seven fraternity houses and one scholarship hall became their sleeping quarters, and the Kansas Union their mess hall.

The Navy also took over the west wing and entire top floor of Strong Hall for use as a dormitory and baths for several hundred uniformed sailors who underwent four-month courses to become machinist's and electrician's mates. According to *The Graduate Magazine*, the sailors set up clotheslines on the north side of Strong to dry their uniforms. More than 4,000 participated in the program, which lasted until 1944.

Civilian enrollment on the Lawrence campus declined sharply — to 3,430 in 1942 and 3,104 in 1943, bottoming out at 2,425 in fall

1944. But as military programs rented campus space and paid faculty for war training, the total number of young people on campus diminished less rapidly. By accepting military programs, the university not only minimized enrollment losses but also received federal payments.

Because of war-related delays of construction materials the mineral resources building, approved by the Legislature in spring 1941 and named for the late chancellor Ernest Lindley that summer, did not open until summer 1943. When it did, most of its space was claimed by the military. Lindley Hall became a dormitory and mess hall for U.S. Army trainees, numbering up to 800, under what the military called the Army Specialized Training Program. Not until

Navy V-12 candidates, some still in civilian clothes and all at attention.

On the eve of war, students, all in civilian dress, jammed the sidewalks along Jayhawk Boulevard.

February 1946 would Lindley be converted fully to its intended use.

The military also got its own permanent structure, the Military Science Building for the ROTC. The building was begun with federal money and finished in 1943 with funds from the state and the KU Endowment Association.

War programs also affected the School of Medicine in Kansas City, Kansas, where four of five doctors in training were mustered into programs allowing them to remain in school and afterward become Navy or Army physicians. In fall 1943, enrollment there exceeded 400, an unprecedented number.

By late 1944, America and the Allies were meeting marked success in the war and campus military programs began winding down. Early 1945 found only about 400 students in military programs still on campus. That spring, the first sign of postwar things to come arrived: Seventy discharged veterans enrolled.

Already, KU officials projected that enrollment after the war would reach 6,000, creating a shortage of classroom capacity on campus and severe problems with housing. Events would show they guessed low, by two to three thousand students.

The expansive postwar era was about to

The Military Science Building, new home for ROTC.

begin. In Europe, war came to an end with German surrender in May 1945. After the United States dropped two atomic bombs, Japan surrendered in September. At KU that same month, almost 300 veterans enrolled; 120 of them married. They marked only the beginning of times unlike any the university had known.

Aftermath of war

With the war's end, the University of Kansas surged in nearly every way. Returning veterans filled everything to overflowing. Older and more experienced than the traditional college-age student, the veterans brought with them more serious attitudes. With them also came government compensation payments.

As did the national economy, the Kansas economy converted to a peacetime footing with no serious downturn. State revenues rose and the Legislature turned a kind eye toward KU's budget requests. Even the football team, for two decades only a sometime winner, headed for its first bowl game.

In the first full year of peace, 1946, enrollment on the Lawrence campus more than doubled from the year before, topping 8,600. In fall 1948 it exceeded 9,300, straining the campus,

while the Medical School hit a record 426. Of the 1948 total, veterans numbered almost 4,800.

The total teaching staff, counting assistant instructors, reached 1,000 that year and 1,200 the next. Still, they faced an onslaught; in each of 12 basic economics classes, 105 students were enrolled. Two beginning philosophy classes had 225 students each.

The federal GI Bill offered money for tuition and expenses. Service veterans took advantage; before the war, many of them might have skipped college.

Faculty found the former soldiers and sailors mature, thoughtful and dedicated to their classwork. Meanwhile, according to Clifford Griffin in *The University of Kansas: A History*, they "stayed away in droves" from university and class dances and disappointed Lawrence tavern owners with their poor patronage. On the other hand, they flooded apartment and rooming houses.

Chancellor Malott welcomed the deluge.

"The University of Kansas will not turn down a single applicant for enrollment," he told Lawrence business people in 1946, "as long as there is a room, garret, basement, attic, cellar or warehouse left in Lawrence that can be made into a decent place to live."

To that end, KU asked Lawrence residents to make room in their homes for students. The offices of the advisors of men and women served as a clearinghouse and occasionally as a watchdog over landlords who tried to gouge desperate tenants.

In the basement of the Spooner-Thayer Museum of Art, plywood partitions were set up to create a study area, showers and a bunk room for 80 men. To former servicemen, that was still an improvement over what they had experienced in the war. Still more students bunked in hastily arranged quarters under Memorial Stadium and at a downtown church. Hundreds of other veterans and their families found living space in now-vacant quarters at the Sunflower munitions plant 13 miles east. Because many of the veterans were married, space had to be found for spouses

Makeshift recreation hall at the Med Center in 1947.

and, before long, children.

Emergency classroom buildings went up, numbering about a dozen by fall 1948. Some were simple corrugated-metal Quonset huts. All this only delayed a solution to the crowding problem. Indeed, the university found that the skyrocketing enrollments provided a sound and persuasive argument for more money from the state for buildings, not to mention more faculty.

Because of the compensatory fees from the federal government, Chancellor Malott said, the university calculated that a veteran brought KU more than three times as much income as a non-veteran.

Meanwhile the federal government delivered tens of thousands and soon hundreds of thousands of dollars in grants for research in science and medicine. By 1949, the investment surpassed $400,000, and more than 150 persons were working on research projects backed by grants.

Faculty in general saw salaries rise after 1947, the product of good times generally and particularly for Kansas wheat farmers as prices boomed. Manufacturing increased, too, notably in aircraft production in the Wichita area.

In 1945, the university had asked the Legislature for $4.9 million and received about $4.7 million, despite efforts by Governor Andrew Schoeppel to trim the appropriation further. In 1949, with the economy humming — along with

inflation — the two-year grant rose to nearly $6.7 million. Money from the state Educational Building Fund added an additional $1.1 million. Additional income poured in from the federal government and from student fees.

In the year the war ended, all these totaled $4.5 million; four years later they had rocketed to $11 million, not counting a special grant of more than $3.8 million to the Medical Center.

Good times on the field and court

The big hurrah of the immediate postwar years was the Jayhawk football team, which fought its way to prominence, even if only briefly. Under new coach George Sauer, the 1946 team tied for first place in the Big Six Conference, the Jayhawks' best showing since 1930. The 1947 team improved on that. KU's first two All-America players, Ray Evans and Otto Schnellbacher, along

In the basement of the Spooner-Thayer Museum of Art, plywood partitions were set up to create a study area, showers and a bunk room for 80 men. To former servicemen, this was still an improvement over what they had experienced in the war.

with a transfer lineman and placekicker named Don Fambrough led the team to eight wins, two ties and no losses.

Again co-champions of the Big Six, the '47 Jayhawks ended the season on New Year's Day 1948 in the Orange Bowl against Georgia Tech. It was the first bowl game in KU history, but ended disappointingly for the team and the fans who traveled to Miami to watch. Trailing, 20-14, in the closing minutes of the fourth quarter, the Jayhawks lost a fumble at the goal line and with it a chance at victory.

Memorial Stadium filled up in 1947 for the Missouri game. KU won, 20-14, and headed for the Orange Bowl.

Afterward Sauer departed to coach the Naval Academy, and in the 1950s KU reverted to its prewar football pattern: a few good years, a few bad and a few mediocre. There would be no more conference championships until the late 1960s.

The same would not be true of Phog Allen's basketball team. Come war or peace, the Jayhawk basketball team of the 1940s usually acquitted itself superbly. In its third decade under Allen as coach, KU won or tied for five championships in the Big Six Conference, which became the Big Seven in 1948. As the 1950s began, things got even better for the Jayhawks. In 1950, the team tied for first in the conference and in 1951, it tied for second.

In 1952 the Jayhawks won it all. First

came the regular season, which the Jayhawks completed with 22 victories and only two losses, gaining the Big Seven championship. That led to Kansas City, where KU played two rounds of NCAA tournament games. In the early 1950s, only 16 teams qualified for the tournament, so the Jayhawk victories over TCU and St. Louis University advanced the team to the national semifinal game at the University of Washington's arena in Seattle. On March 25, the Jayhawks made it easily past the University of California at Santa Clara, 74-55. The next night they beat Saint John's University of New York, 80-63, for the national championship. KU's star player in the game, as he had been all season, was All-America Clyde Lovellete, a six-foot nine-inch "gentle giant" from

Coach Allen with his 1952 starters. Clyde Lovellette stood to his right. When the Jayhawks played for the NCAA title in Seattle, students watched on televisions set up in the Kansas Union ballroom, below.

Terre Haute, Indiana. He scored 33 points.

In Lawrence, students gathered at the Kansas Union, which had set up televisions for the occasion, or listened on the radio. The game ended well after 1 a.m. Central time, and hundreds of people whooped and hollered their way to a spontaneous pep rally at 10th and Massachusetts streets. The team returned to Lawrence late the next night after a flight delay, but still were greeted by thousands of fans. Atop a fire truck that escorted the procession stood Lovellette, never bashful, wearing a fireman's hat.

Lovellette was a senior that year, but even without him in the 1952-53 season the Jayhawks nearly did it all again. With B.H. Born as center and leading scorer, KU won the Big Seven, beat

Oklahoma City and Oklahoma State in the Midwest Regional and coasted past the University of Washington in the semifinal game in Kansas City. In the national championship, however, KU lost by one point to Indiana University.

Veterans depart and the campus gets bigger

With the graduation of veterans, KU enrollments receded. On the Lawrence campus, the number of students dropped to about 8,300 in fall 1949, one thousand fewer than the year before. University revenues slowed as compensatory payments for veterans ran out and the national economy underwent a mild downturn. Still, there was money for general research, some of it granted for the first time by the state of Kansas.

Enrollment, however, remained well above its prewar peaks and the campus continued to grow briskly. Watson Library added two wings in late 1949 to hold several large new collections of books on natural history, economics and other topics. Holdings now totaled 600,000-plus volumes. New engineering shops, named Fowler like the ones they replaced, were ready for use in 1950. The Kansas Union sprouted additions in 1948 and again in the early 1950s.

The old Fowler Shops were remodeled to house the new William Allen White School of Journalism and Public Information, promoted from department to a two-year school in 1948 and renamed for the renowned Emporia editor. Since 1923, student journalists had worked in the old Chemistry Building of the early 1880s — known colloquially as "the shack" for the shed-roofed wooden extension attached to it. Journalism's new home was renamed Flint Hall in 1952 after longtime instructor Leon Flint.

As a memorial to the 276 KU students and alumni who died in World War II and in honor of the thousands who served, the university built a campanile and bell tower. Dedicated May 21,

Flint Hall, converted for journalism classes.

1951, the tower instantly became a landmark for the eye and the ear along the new Memorial Drive, which wound along the northern slope of Mount Oread. Inside the tower was a 53-bell carillon, on which concerts could be played. The rest of the time the bells rang out the quarter-hour, half-hour and hour. The campanile was built primarily from contributions with some help from the Legislature.

Three new scholarship halls — in which residents did various chores in return for lower rent — were built from money donated by Joseph R. Pearson and his wife, Gertrude Sellards Pearson. Pearson Hall for men opened in 1945; Sellards and Grace Pearson for women opened in 1952 and 1955, respectively. In 1960, Grace Pearson became a men's scholarship hall. Stephenson Hall for men opened in 1951 and Douthart Hall for women — built on the site of the original chancellor's residence — in 1954. Scholarship halls clustered in the southeast part of campus.

The Pearsons also contributed to a new women's dormitory named for her, which opened near Corbin and the site of Old North College in 1955, and to a men's dormitory named for him, which opened in 1959 on the northwest corner of

New war, new memorial

Plans for a tower in memory of KU's World War II dead were drawn as early as 1946, right. By 1951, the final design was constructed. Enormous bells were installed to toll the hours. The largest weighed seven tons.

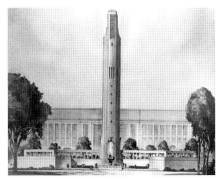

Bells also formed a carillon inside the tower. The carillonneur sounded notes by striking wooden handles.

After the last construction towers were removed, the Memorial Campanile was dedicated in May 1951.

the main campus.

Of the postwar projects the smallest but one of the most notable was a nondenominational chapel, constructed between Fraser and Spooner-Thayer and named for William H. Danforth of Ralston Purina fame in St. Louis. Danforth, whose foundation helped build similar chapels at various colleges and who already provided fellowships for doctoral students, made the largest contribution, but students, faculty and alumni also donated. The building was begun while the war was still under way by German prisoners of war who had been captured in North Africa and who were held in a facility near the Santa Fe station in Lawrence. It was one of 14 POW camps that dotted Kansas. Danforth Chapel was dedicated in April 1946. In years to come, it would host many a wedding for students, graduates and friends of KU.

The campus flora improved in the early 1950s, too. The chancellor's wife, Eleanor Malott, and a planning committee campaigned for donations of plantings. Among the new trees were more than 1,200 flowering crabapples given by the class of 1945.

Another chancellor, another alumnus

Chancellor Malott established a record of success with the Kansas Legislature. He won long-awaited salary increases for faculty, some approaching 50 percent. He also won approval for yet more buildings, in particular two large additions to the campus map. One would house the chemistry, pharmacy and physics departments. Completed in 1954, the university named it Malott Hall in his honor. The other was a new fieldhouse for track and field, concerts and other uses, but most of all for Phog Allen's basketball team.

Before the fieldhouse and Malott Hall opened, however, Dean Malott moved on. In January 1951, he announced that he would become president of Cornell University in

Danforth Chapel, built in 1946, was and is a popular site for campus weddings.

New York, and he departed that June. He had persevered through the disruptions and shortages of wartime and then through the plenty of peacetime, and got good marks from most faculty, students and alumni.

Fred Ellsworth of the Alumni Association called him "one of the greatest salesmen Kansas ever had." Malott agreed with the description.

Malott Hall in 1954.

"I always had my tambourine out for funds," he said. "I found the Legislature very much interested in higher education. They wanted to be proud of their university and it was my job to make them proud of it."

Malott said he and his wife "have spent 12 very busy and very happy years, and we have somehow built ourselves into KU."

On July 2, 1951, the regents chose as a new chancellor, Franklin D. Murphy Jr. Murphy had strong connections to the university. His father had headed the Kansas City Medical College, one of three schools in the Kansas City area that merged in 1905 into the KU School of Medicine. The new chancellor graduated from KU in 1936 and received his medical degree from the University of Pennsylvania, where he was class valedictorian. After his discharge from the Army

in 1946, Murphy joined the KU Medical School, which was renamed the KU Medical Center the next year. In 1948 Murphy, then only 32 years old, was made dean.

He was credited with inspiring statewide support of the Medical Center through the Rural Health Program for Kansas, which aimed to provide doctors for areas of the state that had few or none. Most of those areas were rural. With Murphy's urging, the Kansas Farm Bureau and several newspapers fell in behind what became known as the Murphy Plan. In turn, the state provided the Medical Center money for new facilities. The result brought Murphy respect for his leadership and political savvy from administrators, alumni and state officials.

Despite Murphy's age of 35, the youngest chancellor in university history, he was a

The KU Medical Center in Kansas City, Kansas, as it appeared from above in 1951.

nearly universal choice to succeed Malott. To succeed himself at the Medical Center, Murphy handpicked W. Clarke Wescoe, a professor of pharmacology.

Enrollment in Murphy's first year, 1951, dipped to 6,000 on the Lawrence campus. From that point, it climbed past 8,000 again in 1956 and kept growing. At the Medical Center, enrollment only grew, reaching 500 in Murphy's first year as chancellor, surpassing 600 the next year and 700 the year after that.

As chancellor, Murphy proved thoughtful, articulate and — through his first five years — reasonably effective at getting resources for the university. The Board of Regents cooperated and a succession of Republican governors argued little with the university and its administration. Nevertheless, Murphy and others at KU believed that the state alone would never give the

university all it needed to achieve greatness.

"If we are to do those special things that add uniqueness and distinction to high quality, we must turn to the host of friends and alumni of the university," the chancellor said. He thus declared private giving the key to the future.

Franklin D. Murphy

In 1953, the alumni and endowment associations joined efforts to create the Greater University Fund, which would harvest money for scholarships, collections of fine art and books and more. In its first year, the fund raised about $42,000 from more than 1,600 alumni and friends. The Endowment Association prospered through the decade and beyond, its assets rising from $3.8 million in 1951 to more

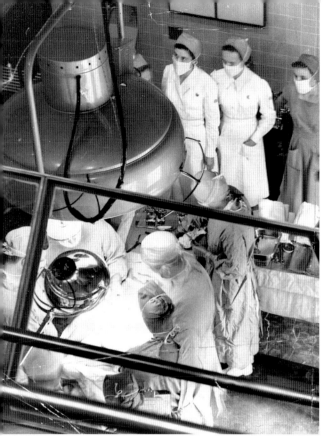

Surgery at KU Med in 1949 with students looking on.

The enrollment board in 1955. Below, a psychology class filled the room in 1958.

than $8.25 million in 1959. One result was multiple endowed professorships.

Students and their parents contributed, too, through increasing tuition. The higher cost of a KU degree did not, however, curb enrollments. In 1960, for the first time since the postwar surge of 1948, fall enrollment topped 9,000 on the Lawrence campus. More than 700 enrolled at the Medical Center.

That same year, KU's income reached more than $28 million. Slightly more than half came from state appropriations and thus from taxpayers throughout Kansas. Nearly $2 million came from fees at the Lawrence campus and more than $300,000 from the Medical Center. The rest came from gifts, grants and endowment income.

Continuing growth of the American middle class, the relative peace of the Eisenhower era and a stable economy helped KU's prospects through the period. And surely, excitement over KU's athletic program, and particularly its basketball team, did nothing to hurt them.

Wilt the Stilt

In 1955, in the middle of his fourth decade as coach, Phog Allen saw a dream realized. Never satisfied with the restrictions imposed by playing on the floor in Hoch Auditorium, Allen for years had wished publicly that KU would build a palace for basketball. First the Depression interfered. Then World War II and even the Korean War got in the way of money and construction materials. After Kansas State got on the road to its own new arena, KU and Allen increased their efforts.

The result was a huge, limestone-faced indoor stadium — second largest on any American campus after Minnesota's — that rose to the south of Mount Oread. It faced a street that had been named Naismith Drive after Allen's coach, the inventor of basketball. It opened in time for the last game of the 1954-1955 Jayhawk basketball season, against Kansas State.

The team that year posted one of the worst records of Phog Allen's long coaching career, winning 11 games and losing 10 and had not won a single home game in Hoch.

On March 1, 1955, an announced crowd of 17,228 attended the game that marked the opening of the arena, named Allen Fieldhouse. At the half-hour-long halftime ceremony, the Alumni Association handed Allen the keys to a new Cadillac. In the game itself, KU vanquished its cross-state rivals, 77-67.

One reason Allen hungered for the new building was the effect it might have on recruits, and evidently the effect was superb. In summer 1955, Allen succeeded in recruiting Wilt Chamberlain, a towering, quick and wonderfully coordinated player from Philadelphia whom many declared would turn into the greatest basketball player in America.

Despite that success, however, Allen coached Chamberlain only in his freshman year, when the rules of the era banned freshman from varsity competition. Before Chamberlain's sophomore year, Allen turned 70 years old, which was the mandatory retirement age for state employees. In early March 1956, Allen asked publicly to stay on one more year to coach a team he believed would be "truly great." The KU Athletic Board, consisting of administrators, faculty, alumni and students, turned him down, choosing not to make an exception to the retirement rule. It recommended to the regents instead that the university replace Allen with Dick Harp, Allen's assistant coach, and the idea was approved. Harp played at KU under Allen from 1938 to 1940.

In the 1956-57 season, behind Chamberlain's 29.6 points a game, the Jayhawks finished first in the Big Seven and fought past SMU and Oklahoma City in the Midwest Regional

Wilt Chamberlain scoring in 1956. The opponents could only watch.

in Dallas. That brought them to Kansas City for the semifinal game, where they beat San Francisco, 80-56, and faced North Carolina for the championship. The teams played through the regulation time and three overtimes before North Carolina eked out a narrow victory, 53-54. The next year, Chamberlain's final season, KU compiled an 18-5 record while "Wilt the Stilt" averaged 30.1 points a game. Then Chamberlain left to play for the Harlem Globetrotters.

The feud

As the basketball team prospered and the university kept growing, the work of Franklin Murphy ground to a halt, partly because of his own doing. In late summer and fall

Phog Allen showed off plans for the fieldhouse of his dreams to Kansas Governor Frank Carlson, right.

1956 Murphy campaigned openly for the GOP candidate for governor. Murphy was a Republican — traditionally a common affiliation in Kansas — like all of his predecessors. None of the previous chancellors, however, had worked quite so openly to boost a candidate. In 1956 Murphy's candidate was Warren W. Shaw, and the chancellor took pains to remind Kansans of all the good that Republicans had done for the university since the end of the war. He went further, denigrating Shaw's opponents on the Democratic side for what he called their poverty of ideas and programs.

Despite Murphy's best effort, Shaw went down to defeat and the victor, a Democrat named George Docking, did not forget what the chancellor had done. In Docking's first year as governor, 1957, he trimmed KU's request for appropriations, asked for a survey of the educational system by outside experts and began questioning travel subsidies for faculty, at one point canceling some faculty travel.

The last move affected two anatomy professors of seven from KU who had planned to attend a meeting of their professional association in Baltimore. Although the state would still pay the way for the remaining five, Murphy could not keep silent, saying, "In any field you cannot keep up very long by locking yourself in a closet."

Unfazed by the criticism, Docking continued on his path. He pushed the Board of Regents to review all the programs at state-supported institutions of higher education and in particular the extent of research. His aim,

In 1958, sculptor Eldon Teft's Jayhawk was placed in the Union.

debate between the two men.

In a February 1959 interview with *The University Daily Kansan*, Docking called KU a "trouble spot." At the root of the problem, he said in a thinly veiled jab at Murphy, was the close tie between university administrators and the Republican Party. In early 1960 Docking told a meeting of Democrats in Great Bend, Kansas, that the chancellor was making $22,000 "plus a free house, a free car and overseas junkets paid by the federal government."

"I think he's getting enough," the governor said. "We can get plenty of others as good for less."

The *Jayhawker* yearbook typically contained pages for scores of campus clubs and in the text of its 1960 display of the campus Young Republicans it wrote: "Democratic Governor George Docking has unknowingly brought on both a larger and more active membership in the club than has previously been realized."

On March 16, 1960, Murphy, then 44, announced that he was resigning the KU job as of July 1 and taking over as chancellor of the University of California at Los Angeles. Surprised supporters would not make him change his mind. The decision, he said, was made only after much soul-searching.

"I have shared the pride of the state...in what I believe has been modest progress at the

the governor said, was to distinguish between spending that contributed to education and "those things which though desirable may represent luxuries which the taxpayers cannot afford." He also asked the regents to eliminate duplication, to examine salaries and perhaps to raise admission requirements.

Again Murphy did not hold back, complaining to newspapers about politicians "who evidently think Kansas can afford only a mediocre university."

The constant political boxing created suspicions that the dispute between Docking and Murphy was personal. In public both denied it, but associates of Docking quoted the governor as calling Murphy, among other things, "that little punk."

Throughout the disputes, the university continued to win support from the Republican-dominated Legislature. Session after session, Docking recommended cuts in KU's budget and session after session the Legislature restored them. That did not lower the temperature of the

The combatants: Governor Docking, left, and Murphy. Docking's wife, Virginia Docking, stood between them on this occasion.

Students of the middle 1950s, several in ROTC uniforms, crossed the hillside near Malott Hall.

university during these years," he said, "progress achieved in spite of unreasonable and, indeed, unprecedented handicaps."

The next evening, hundreds of students gathered on the snow-covered lawn at the chancellor's residence, chanting, "We want Murphy!" and also carrying effigies of the governor and signs, one of which read "To Hell with Docking! Stay Here Murphy."

Murphy appeared briefly, saying: "Ever since I've held this position here it hasn't been a job to me at all, but a sort of love affair. Thank you and God bless you all."

One of the regents, Claude Bradney of Columbus, Kansas, said: "I don't blame him for getting out of Kansas and away from Docking. I guess he just got tired of the abuse."

On March 18, almost 4,000 students crowded Hoch Auditorium for a protest meeting. There were calls to stage a protest in Topeka, but Murphy urged the students to cool down. He hoped, he said, that his departure would end with a "clearing of the atmosphere."

The 1960 *Jayhawker* staff dedicated the yearbook to the departing chancellor.

"By his resignation," the editor wrote, "a deep feeling of loss was sensed from freshman to professor, from the most emotional to the most intellectual."

High on the list of candidates to replace Murphy was the dean of the Medical School, W. Clarke Wescoe. Wescoe, Pennsylvania-born and educated, received his medical training at Cornell University Medical College in New York City. After Pearl Harbor, he entered the Army Specialized Training Program, which chose high-performance students for officer training. In 1944, he married KU graduate and Kansas City native Barbara Benton, whom he had met when her father presented him a national fraternity honor.

After his discharge from the Army, Wescoe went to work on the pharmacology faculty at Cornell. There he won a research fellowship that was noticed by then-medical dean Franklin Murphy, who hired Wescoe for the faculty in 1950. In July 1952 Wescoe became dean. He was 32 years old, the same age as Murphy when he entered the job. In the new job, Wescoe shone,

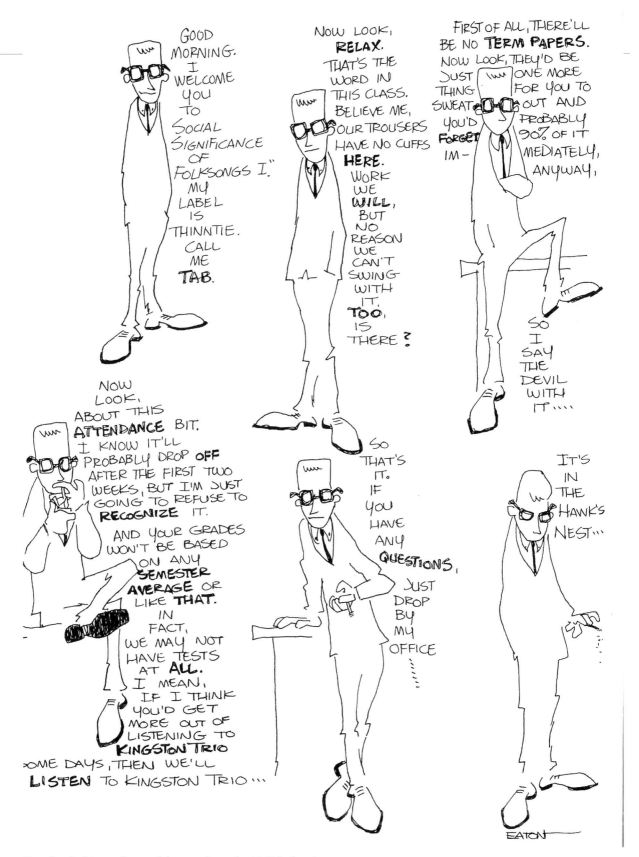

Parody of a hip professor of the era, from the 1961 Jayhawker.

carrying out Murphy's plan to send doctors to underserved parts of Kansas. By 1958, Wescoe declared that every Kansan was within 20 minutes by car of good medical care.

On March 21, 1960, only four days after Murphy's resignation, the regents put Wescoe's name to a vote. For the departing Murphy, Governor Docking had one last fusillade, instructing his appointees on the board to vote "no" to Wescoe. Three of the four Docking appointees did so, but they were in the minority and Wescoe won the job by a vote of six to three.

The meeting took five minutes. Wescoe would recall that within a week the Docking appointees apologized for their votes.

Wescoe was 39 when he took office on July 1, 1960. Four months later, George Docking lost his bid for election to a third term.

W. Clarke Wescoe

Bright and shiny, south and west

With a perspective tinged by modernism, the winter installment of the 1962 *Jayhawker* remarked: "The University of Kansas has two campuses. One, on the eastern side of Mt. Oread, is old, traditional, covered with vines and grime. The other, to the south and west is new, modern shiny."

Like much architecture of the day, KU's newest buildings faced the world with a skin of brick or smooth limestone mostly free of ornament.

Obvious by its massive presence on the south side of Mount Oread, the new music and dance building sprawled, faced with light-colored brick and limestone. It opened in 1957, and was KU's first building dedicated to the performing arts. After Chancellor Murphy's departure in 1960, it was named for him. Murphy Hall

contained performance halls, rehearsal spaces, offices for faculty and for the School of Fine Arts administration, and practice rooms.

Next to Murphy and marked by a south-facing glass façade, Summerfield Hall went up. Summerfield housed the School of Business, the economics department and a computer center. It opened in 1959. Across Sunnyside Drive from Summerfield, the university in 1966 would construct a new health and physical education building named Robinson, and next to that in 1969 a center for biological sciences that would be named Haworth Hall. The names of two buildings that would be demolished at the top of the hill thus were placed on the two new structures. In 1963 came a new engineering building, Learned Hall.

The late 1950s and 1960s turned KU into a landlord as well as educator, providing room and board for thousands of students who in earlier years would have found quarters only in boarding houses, residences that had been converted to small dormitories or scholarship halls.

In September 1955, KU opened the 200-bed Carruth-O'Leary Hall as a men's dormitory. Six-story Joseph R. Pearson, which could hold 416 men, went into service in spring 1959 at the northwest corner of campus.

To the west, atop Daisy Hill and flanking Iowa Street, the university opened a series of high-rise, red-brick dormitories. Each had elevators carrying students to floors with common rooms leading to long halls and double-occupancy bedrooms. First came Templin Hall, which opened in September 1959 at Iowa and

Murphy Hall in 1957.

Summerfield Hall in 1960.

Gertrude Sellards Pearson residence hall.

15th streets, and then its partner, Lewis Hall, which opened in February 1960. In the beginning each was a men's dorm, seven stories tall, with a capacity of more than 430.

After them came Hashinger Hall for junior and senior women, capacity 436, in 1962. Ellsworth Hall, which could hold 620 men, arose in 1963. McCollum, KU's first large co-ed dorm with a capacity of more than 900 students in 10 stories, was opened in spring 1965. Oliver Hall for women opened in 1966 at the southern end of campus, Naismith Drive and 19th Street.

KU would need all the dormitories it could muster, because population projections showed a coming wave of students representing the Baby Boom, the legion of young people born after World War II who were now reaching college age. They would need not only places to live but also classrooms and laboratories.

So with the building of the new and "shiny" campus on acres of vacant land, the university also turned to appraising the future of structures on the old, "vine-covered" campus. To the chagrin of a segment of alumni and students, the review would end in destruction of a nine-decade-old landmark.

First, however, went old Blake Hall, demolished in 1963. The next year, in its place up went new Blake, which little resembled its predecessor. The same year, the old Chemistry Building of the 1880s, long since forsaken

Two residence halls opened across campus from one another in 1959, J.R. Pearson, above, and Templin, below.

Mixed fortune in football, missed chance in NCAAs

In the late 1950s and early 1960s under Coach Jack Mitchell, the stars came out for KU football. One was quarterback/halfback John Hadl, a Lawrence native who went on to a long professional career. Another was running back Curtis McClinton of Wichita, who later played for the Kansas City Chiefs.

With them in the backfield, the Jayhawks never won the conference but won more games than they lost. The most memorable victory, one still in dispute, came in the final game of the 1960 season against then No. 1-ranked Missouri in Columbia. KU upset the Tigers, 23-7, probably costing Missouri the national championship. Afterward, the Big Eight Conference ruled that KU back Bert Coan had violated NCAA rules by receiving a free plane ride from a KU alum, and the game was forfeited, although KU still claims the victory in its season record. The next year Hadl, McClinton and the rest of the 1961 squad received the second bowl invitation in KU history. In the Bluebonnet Bowl in Houston they beat Rice, 33-7.

After their departure, the next three seasons featured running back Gale Sayers, the "Kansas Comet," and his spectacular running. Among Sayers' accomplishments were a 99-yard run against Nebraska and a 96-yard kickoff return against Oklahoma. Sayers' accumulation of yardage from the backfield and returning kickoffs and punts made him an All-America. He went on to play for the Chicago Bears, leading the National Football League in rushing in 1966 and 1969.

Basketball, after the end of the Wilt Chamberlain era in 1958, occasionally struggled — at least, based on KU's high standards. In 1958-1959, the Jayhawks fell to 11 wins and 14 losses but tied for the conference championship in 1959-60 season. After that, the team recorded a series of conference finishes ranging from second to seventh place and posted mediocre records. After the 1963-64 season 1964 KU fired Coach Dick Harp, Phog Allen's former assistant.

In his place KU hired a young graduate of the University of Oklahoma, Ted Owens, who recruited an outstanding point guard, Jo Jo White, from St. Louis. In 1965-1966, Owens' sec-

The Jayhawk mascot fired up fans by kicking a Missouri tiger in 1967.

ond year, the Jayhawks climbed back atop the Big Eight Conference and advanced to the final game of the NCAA Midwest Regional in Lubbock, Texas, against an upstart team, Texas Western. With the game tied and the final seconds of overtime ticking away, White launched a shot from the left sideline that went in, apparently giving KU the victory and a trip to the final four. But the referee waved off the attempt, saying that one of White's feet had crossed the out-of-bounds line. In the second overtime, Texas Western won the game and went on to beat Kentucky for the national championship.

Gale Sayers, All-America running back.

Curtis McClinton.

John Hadl.

by chemists and occupied for decades by a succession of other departments, was demolished to make room for an expansion of Watson Library. And then there was Fraser Hall.

"Sound the crowbars!"

Every college-level graduating class since the first one in 1873 had known Fraser. When it opened it was KU's pride and joy. For years the twin-towered building represented all there was of the University of Kansas, and everything that happened at KU happened in it. Tens of thousands of students enrolled in it, took classes in it, studied in it and performed in it. Yet from early in its history, the building had shown weakness.

State Architect John G. Haskell, who designed the structure, examined it himself in 1885, when the hall was only 12 years old and still named University Hall. His review described the foundation as in "very bad condition." Water seeped in and cracks already had appeared in the walls. The university commissioned a quick repair, which bought time for the building, but slowly its innards and its reputation deteriorated. In 1923, a faculty report found more structural problems. Also it complained about rats and mice, splintered floors "impregnated with dirt," poor ventilation and lighting and unreliable heating.

Through the years, things only grew worse.

In February 1962, after considerable study, Chancellor Wescoe and the regents announced that Fraser had "outlived its usefulness." KU's signature building, he said, was "being kept usable only at unusual expense." Anticipating objections, he cited estimates showing that salvaging Fraser could cost twice as much as building a new one. Plans called for the old building to go down within five years.

Upon hearing the news, Theodore M. O'Leary journeyed to Lawrence to visit Fraser, which he remembered from his own days as a student in the 1930s and from earlier years, when

Another dorm for Daisy Hill. Hashinger in 1961.

his father taught there.

"As…I climbed the ornately carved mahogany stairways, the treads creaked just as they had creaked when I had climbed them 30 years ago," O'Leary wrote in *The Kansas City Star.* "There was the same familiar smell of floor oil. The interior walls were crisscrossed with scores of recently applied patches intended to fill in cracks in the plaster."

In March 1965, KU unveiled a model of a bigger, boxy structure proposed to replace Fraser. Wescoe pointed to two towers and flagpoles that architects had planted atop the new building and remarked that "plans for the new Fraser Hall provide a remarkable combination of the traditional and the functional." State Architect James C. Canole drew the new building along with a retired Topeka architect, T.R. Griest.

Their work drew a new round of complaints.

"I swear to you I've found no one who likes

In February 1962, after considerable study, Chancellor Wescoe and the regents announced that Fraser had "outlived its usefulness."

Talking and studying, students staged a fair housing sit-in outside the chancellor's office in 1965.

Sitting in to root out discrimination

All through the 1950s and into the early 1960s, the university watched as the civil rights movement took on Jim Crow laws, the deeply entrenched ordinances separating races in the Deep South. Besides legal action, the movement used marches, sit-ins and other public demonstrations, usually peaceful, to make its case.

On March 8,1965, civil rights demonstrators took on the University of Kansas over the question of fair housing. In a 90-minute meeting with Chancellor Wescoe, they demanded he sign an executive order ordering fraternities and sororities to abolish discrimination by race and to refuse advertising space in KU publications to individuals or groups who discriminated. When Wescoe rejected their proposal, the demonstrators staged a silent sit-down in the hallway of Strong Hall outside his office.

Wescoe told the group not to block the halls and to leave by 10 p.m., when the building would be locked for the night. Late that night, he suspended 114 demonstrators, who were also booked by the police on charges of trespassing and disturbing the peace. All paid $25 bonds and many returned to Strong Hall the next day.

Meanwhile, the All Student Council passed a measure outlawing discriminatory clauses in the constitutions of campus organizations, and Wescoe signed it. A week later, the council voted to forbid KU publications from discriminating. On March 19, the Board of Regents adopted a proposal affirming that the regents opposed discrimination. It went on to say the regents expected administrators to defend "responsible exercise" of speech, assembly and petition, but also to preserve peace and prevent disruption of educational functions.

By June, KU administrators had decided not to press charges and to reinstate the suspended students. With that, a brief surge of mid-1960s civil rights protest receded. But unrest over various issues would return to the campus and the city around it within a few years.

the new building," said Bernard Frazier, sculptor-in-residence at KU and member of a group opposing demolition. "I am sure that a vote in the entire architectural profession would show not even 5 percent in favor of the design."

Yet the project rumbled on. Already, the balcony of the auditorium was closed and plans called for old Fraser to be razed soon after the end of the spring term in 1965. Announcement of the timetable spurred new efforts by those who wanted to save the old building. In June preservationists called on the governor to place a 60-day moratorium on demolition plans. The structure could be saved and reworked as a museum or archive, they said.

A member of the Save Old Fraser Committee, William J. Sollner, wrote a poem lamenting the possibility. It was published in *The Kansas City Star.*

> *Sound the crowbars!*
> *Ring the axes!*
> *It's no longer worth the taxes,*
> *And our Kansas is so poor*
> *And the past is such a bore.*
> *Let no trace of it remain,*
> *Not a panel, sash, or pane,*
> *Not a door, or window frame,*
> *To remind us of our shame.*
> *(All that's beautiful must go,*
> *For the regents tell us so.)*

> *Let us raze historic halls!*
> *Never mind what duty calls.*
> *They are too old – their people cold –*
> *Engrossed in gain – the story's old.*
> *Reduce them first, of course, to tatters:*
> *Progress! Progress! That's what matters.*
> *To regents' minds that's obvious,*
> *If not so to – the rest of us.*
> *(All that's beautiful must go,*
> *For the regents tell us so.)*

The objections came to naught. In August 1965, the wrecking ball reduced old Fraser to a heap of rubble. True to the surveys, wreckers found no real foundations, only rock walls that extended a mere 12 inches below the basement floor, resting on earth and not on bedrock. The head of the wrecking company said the building was in the worst condition of any he had demolished in 20 years.

In spring 1966, the university celebrated its centennial year with speeches by renowned thinkers and the premiere of an opera, "Carrie Nation." It did so without its longtime signature building.

An architect's model of the new Fraser Hall, west side.

The head of the wrecking company said the building was in the worst condition of any he had demolished in 20 years.

Following pages: On a cool autumn day in 1964, students strolled along Jayhawk Boulevard under a canopy of elms.

End of an era

After nine decades atop the hill a badly deteriorated Fraser Hall, once the pride of KU, fell to the wrecking crew in August 1965.

An Era of Trial and Tumult

In the middle 1960s, the age of public protest arrived at the University of Kansas. Beginning with sit-ins at Strong Hall and silent peace vigils in front of the library, it evolved into larger crowds of demonstrators, some shouting and some marching quietly across campus to make a point.

Their issues ranged from national to intensely local, from the military draft and the war in Southeast Asia to unfair landlords and the conduct of local police.

Students who were passionate about social and political issues divided along cultural and political lines. Protesters disrupted campus events. Someone set fire to the Kansas Union. A bomb exploded at the computer center. One demonstration led to the shooting and wounding of a student in front of the library. When feelings peaked in spring 1970, the university agreed to let students skip the final days of the semester.

Through almost all the commotion of the late 1960s and early 1970s, classes continued as usual. The vast majority of students went to school, did their homework, took their exams and partied on weekends. Graduates left for careers and advanced degrees. Enrollment rose through each year of the turmoil, just as it had every year since 1951. In 1965, more than 13,500 students signed up for the fall semester on the Lawrence campus. In fall 1970, Lawrence campus

Facing page: 1966 traditional — waving the wheat at Memorial Stadium.

1966 non-traditional — sidewalk marchers calling for an end to U.S. military involvement in Vietnam.

enrollment neared 18,000 and by 1974 it would surpass 20,000. Over the long history of the University of Kansas, the turbulent era proved a transitory though memorable episode.

The more outrageous disruptions inflamed some politicians and other public officials, who blamed permissive attitudes by KU administrators for endangering order, property and even life. Yet with time, the hubbub dwindled, the university made rapid strides in buildings, state support and enrollment, and the critics turned to other matters.

A concoction of causes

Strong feelings about political and social events had surfaced occasionally at the University of Kansas over the years, most notably in the late 1930s over communism and pacifism, but they bubbled up largely in articles and arguments in

In the 1960s, forces far larger than the university flowed together, and certain traditions and certainties about American life began to wobble.

the student press. Big crowds gathered rarely over such issues; more common were marches in support of things such as a day off from classes after a key football victory, or a longer Christmas break.

In the 1960s, forces far larger than the university flowed together, and certain traditions and certainties about American life began to wobble.

Robinson Gym was demolished in 1967, making room for Wescoe Hall.

The war in Vietnam dragged on with little visible progress but with the deaths of tens of thousands of American youths, many of them drafted into military service. Not surprisingly an anti-draft movement sprang up among the young. Distaste for the U.S. role in the war intensified distrust of the military-industrial complex and of corporate America.

College students of the 1960s formed part of the largest generation in U.S. history, the postwar Baby Boomers. At KU, enrollment was double what it had been in the late 1940s. In their young lives, the members of this massive generation had seen civil rights demonstrations and civil disobedience, a sexual revolution aided by the birth-control pill, and the spread of marijuana and more powerful drugs into the middle and upper economic strata. Rock music provided a rambunctious and often defiant accompaniment to unrest. Television carried images of free-speech demonstrations on California campuses and in 1967 the "summer of love" in San Francisco.

In Lawrence, as in some other university towns, emerged a subculture variously described as "hippie," "alternative," "counter-culture" or even "freak." It attracted like-minded people from around the country, some of whom enrolled at the university and some of whom did not. Disputes with landlords, teachers and local police bubbled in the same emotional cauldron as the national

The 1970 Jayhawker *yearbook had this farewell for the departing chancellor.*

Demonstrators gave peace signs as ROTC units awaited orders in May 1969. The military review was canceled.

themes.

In spring 1968, student activists in a group called People's Voice sought a greater role for students in running the university, and KU formed a committee to pursue student representation on faculty committees. On September 29, 1968, it proposed a 95-member Student Senate and a University Senate with student members. Five months later, KU students approved the new organization in a campus-wide ballot.

That same month, Chancellor Wescoe surprised the university and most of the public by announcing his resignation. At the university's opening convocation in Hoch Auditorium he said he would leave at the end of the academic year in June 1969 and enter a new career.

"There are times, and I believe this is one," he said, "when a new voice, a new face, a new approach is required."

As for the violence that had broken out on other university campuses, Wescoe said, "Such actions are intolerable in the civilized world and

particularly so on the campus. The power of the intellect has to win out over what we now call quite correctly gut feeling." With that, nearly 60 students who sat near the front of the auditorium walked out, distributing leaflets promoting a meeting of one faction of People's Voice.

Later, Wescoe denied that his stepping down had anything do with student demands or unrest, or with the never-ending struggle with state government over support of higher education. Instead, he pointed to his upcoming 49th birthday and said "it would be a good time to undertake any new endeavors…before I am 50 years old." He had been in demand for other openings — president of the University of Minnesota, chancellor of Indiana University, and head of the American Medical Association. He deflected attempts by members of the Board of Regents to persuade him to reconsider.

After Wescoe finished speaking at the convocation, a packed auditorium rose to give him a standing ovation, one that lasted more than seven minutes. His final months as chancellor,

As part of a program previewing KU for them, freshmen looked around in 1968.

however, would not go easily.

Blocking the show

To middle-of-the road Americans — among them many parents of KU students and most Kansas taxpayers — the Lawrence counterculture remained on the fringe of attention until spring 1969.

On May 9 of that year, the annual Chancellor's Review of ROTC units was preparing to get under way at Memorial Stadium when about 175 anti-war protestors walked on to the field. They sang and chanted and carried signs opposing military influence on campus and the war in Vietnam. Around the reviewing stand they formed a circle, holding hands. Despite requests by officials for them to clear the area, the demonstrators sat down and refused to leave. The ROTC units, whose line of march would have taken them directly into the demonstrators, waited. After 45 minutes of standoff, Chancellor

Wescoe canceled the event. ROTC commanders, he said, told him that under the circumstances holding the review would be impossible.

Administrators had worried about violence; they said that some of the protesters carried baseball bats. In fact, Kansas Highway Patrol and other law enforcement officers waited on the outskirts of Lawrence while the protest was under way. With cancellation of the event, no violence broke out. Thirty-three of the protesters were suspended for a semester and others saw class credits withheld. Among them was the newly elected vice president of the student body.

Wescoe, less than a month before presiding at his last commencement, called the incident "the most disappointing thing that's happened in my 18 years of association with the university."

Across Kansas, politicians and others expressed indignation that the protesters had been allowed to disrupt the review. Wescoe's impending departure meant that the indignation would land on the head of his successor, whom the regents had selected three months earlier with help from an advisory committee of seven students and six faculty members.

E. Laurence Chalmers Jr.

Their choice was E. Laurence Chalmers Jr., a psychologist, graduate of Princeton and a vice president at Florida State University. After his selection, Chalmers was interviewed by a reporter in Tallahassee, where Chalmers had dealt with protesters who occupied a building. That event had ended peacefully.

"I suppose every university has its dissenting students, ranging to the anarchists," Chalmers said. "They simply cannot occupy physical facilities that are needed by other students. Otherwise, they are welcome. The New Left serves to keep us alert to our problem areas, as long as its efforts are not disruptive."

Moratorium day, October 15, 1969: A march through campus and a silent vigil at memorial crosses, right.

Banning certain student groups and activities, he said, was likely to lead to more strident demonstrations than the groups themselves might have staged.

As he began his first semester in September 1969, Chalmers spoke to a group of Kansas City-area community leaders. Although private giving to KU remained overwhelming, he said, state support was becoming shaky. Longtime critics of the university were using the university's tolerance of dissent as a reason to urge cutbacks, even though the university had suspended students after the demonstrations in the spring.

Also in September 1969, KU's new Student Senate met for the first time. It replaced the All Student Council, which in 1943 had combined the Men's Student Council and Women's Student

Government Association. Missing from the Senate meeting was the vice president who had been elected the previous spring. She had participated in the ROTC demonstration and was among those suspended from school.

One month afterward, on October 15, 1969, several thousand people participated in a campus march as part of a nationwide anti-war "Moratorium." Led by a marcher with an American flag and others with a banner reading "Peace Now!" participants walked in column down Jayhawk Boulevard and Memorial Drive. True to the sentiment of the banner, the march went off peacefully and KU passed the winter of 1969-1970 the same way.

A season of turmoil

With the arrival of spring 1970, matters changed. Controversy broke out among the faculty and administration, and violent incidents erupted in Lawrence and on campus. They led to month after month of fire, confrontation and bloodshed.

In early April the Board of Regents delayed the promotion of two professors, one of whom had made a speech attacking the judge in the Chicago Seven trial over riots at the Democratic National Convention in 1968. The other had produced a play deemed obscene by some in Congress. In protest of the delayed promotions, the president of the student body called for a student strike. The action kept few students out of class, and it amounted mainly to a rally at Strong Hall and a concert at Potter Lake. As it happened, on the night of the strike one of the Chicago 7, Abbie Hoffman, spoke at Allen Fieldhouse. He declared the strike a dud and called Lawrence and KU a drag.

The same night, a firebomb was thrown into old Haworth Hall, which was being demolished. In the wee hours of the next morning a pipe bomb exploded near the office of Anchor Savings in Lawrence. Whether or not the events were

related was never discovered, but as April wore on a string of incidents in town and on campus increased the worries of city and KU officials, faculty, students and residents of Lawrence. To many people, it mattered little whether they happened on campus or off and whether there was any evidence that they were connected.

On April 10 the chairman of the campus Black Student Union urged his fellow African-Americans to get firearms to protect themselves from "attempted and threatened violence." At Lawrence High School, protests by black students percolated and on April 13, fifty African-Americans locked themselves into the high school office.

In the middle of those events, the Kappa Sigma fraternity house was set on fire and a downtown furniture store was destroyed by a firebomb.

On Monday night, April 20, the Lawrence School Board heard from about 200 African Americans who argued for more black studies classes at the high school and for more student representation. A resolution calling for the actions was tabled. Later that evening, firebombs were thrown into the windows of the school administration building. Shortly afterward, shots broke windows at East Lawrence glass companies and at the Santa Fe Railroad station.

At 10:38 p.m., a little more than an hour after the firebombs were reported in other parts of Lawrence, the fire department received word that the Kansas Union was on fire.

The blaze began in a sixth-floor restroom and quickly burst through the roof. Seeing the sky alight with flames, student volunteers arrived and helped firefighters stretch hoses into the building. Others retrieved art and other objects as parts of the roof collapsed. Three hours later, after the fire was brought under control, observers could see from the floor of the union ballroom more starry sky than ceiling.

The fire, which caused almost $1 million in

On April 20, 1970, fire broke through the roof of the Kansas Union, lighting the sky. Students helped firemen, left, but damage was extensive, below.

A relieved Chancellor Chalmers in May 1970 after an all-university gathering at the stadium ended peacefully.

damage, was determined to have been set, but no arrests were made. Insurance covered most of the damage and KU was able to reopen the building in August.

The series of disparate and disconcerting events caused Lawrence and Douglas County officials to ask Governor Robert Docking to declare a curfew. He did so on Tuesday, April 21, to begin at 7 p.m. and last until 6 a.m. on the 22nd. In campus buildings, student volunteers joined faculty to watch over things each night. The curfew, its hours shortened each night, lasted four days.

Despite it, violence continued. An apartment building one block from campus on Oread Avenue, already the target of firebombs in earlier days, was torched again. Police dispersed a crowd at the nearby Rock Chalk Cafe, and bricks were thrown at them. The window of the Jayhawk Cafe was smashed and when police arrived they were attacked again with bricks and rocks. Because of the curfew, police worked long shifts, so nearly 30

National Guardsmen were called to help watch the campus.

On April 22, small fires broke out in various spots across KU, one in a trash can near Strong Hall and the other at the ROTC building. Later, police found a board with nails meant to puncture the tires of their patrol cars.

Before emotions could cool, events far away brought them back to a boil. On May 4, at Kent State University in Ohio, four youths demonstrating against the U.S. invasion of Cambodia were shot to death in a confrontation with National Guardsmen. At KU, the ROTC review, disrupted by protests the year before, was canceled to avoid trouble.

Trouble found KU anyway. After an evening rally at Strong Hall to protest the Kent State killings and the invasion of Cambodia, some from the crowd headed down the hill to the ROTC building and threw rocks through its windows. Nearly all windows on the north side were broken.

The next day, the University Senate Executive Committee announced that the university, all students, faculty and administrators, should assemble on May 9 at Memorial Stadium to decide what to do. That day, after some demonstrators were turned back trying to enter the chancellor's office, thousands of students gathered in the west stands of the stadium.

A proposal to allow students to stop taking classes early, skip finals and choose how their grade would be set— under the rubric of "alternatives" — was shouted into approval by the crowd. For students who chose, the spring semester ended early. The university remained technically open, and offered space for discussions and workshops. Disruption took a respite, but only temporarily.

Heat on the head man

On a hot summer night in middle July 1970, Lawrence erupted again. This time, events not only left rules violated and property damaged, but also cost human lives.

The night of the 16th police received reports of gunfire and the wounding of a woman in the 900 block of New York Street on Lawrence's east side. Soon afterward came another report of a shooting and wounding, this one from four blocks away at Afro House, a community center. There, two policeman and a witness saw what they thought might be suspects from the earlier shooting enter Afro House. As the police drove east toward the site of the first shooting, someone fired at their car. Police in a second patrol car saw a man and a woman leave Afro House in a compact automobile. As the police followed, the car speeded up, took a turn too fast and stalled on the sidewalk. A man left the car, ran up the alley between Rhode Island and New Hampshire and, after exchanging shots with the police, was struck by a police bullet.

Dead was 19-year-old Rick "Tiger" Dowdell, formerly a KU freshman. The woman with him was a KU student.

The day after the shooting, a group of black Lawrence residents petitioned the city manager to investigate Dowdell's death. That night, July 17, police and more than 40 African-Americans fired shots at each other near 10th and Pennsylvania in east Lawrence. One policeman was wounded.

Those events ignited days of confrontation and violence that spilled over to the doorstep of KU. Inevitably, they dragged the university back into controversy.

In the neighborhood of 10th Street and Oread Avenue adjoining the campus, trash was set on fire in the street and a building was firebombed. When police and firemen arrived, rocks and bricks were thrown at them. Several score young people headed for Chancellor Chalmers' residence, where a window was broken. In the next several days, the home of a district court judge was firebombed but barely damaged.

On July 20, at 12th and Indiana streets, a fire hydrant was opened and trash set on fire a short distance away. Authorities closed the hydrants, put out the fires and left. An hour and a half later, similar vandalism broke out anew. By then, darkness had fallen and a crowd had gathered at

Lawrence police with helmets and firearms tried to move a crowd on Oread Avenue in July 1970. Days of demonstrations near campus ended in the shooting death of a student from Leawood.

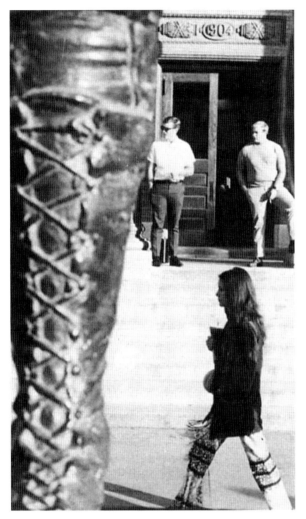

Through the years of protest, most students carried on as always, taking classes, studying and simply hanging out together.

the Rock Chalk Café. When police arrived, people threw rocks, bricks and tomatoes at them. They dispersed the crowd, but the police returned an hour later after receiving reports that the Rock Chalk had been bombed.

By the time they arrived, 150 to 300 people had gathered on Oread Avenue, and several of them overturned a small car in the street. Police advanced, firing tear gas at the crowd. Seeing one person whom they believed was lighting matches to set the overturned car on fire, some policemen also fired their weapons.

A bullet struck one fleeing man, Harry Nick Rice, in the base of the skull. Rice, who lived in Leawood, was a sophomore at KU. A Topeka graduate student was struck by a bullet in the leg.

As bystanders carried the dying Rice into the Gaslight Tavern, police fired more tear gas. In the aftermath, an investigation by the Kansas Bureau of Investigation shed little light on the events of that night and fixed no blame for Rice's death.

Now, Chalmers — less than one year into his job — stood accused of losing control of the situation, even though almost all the events of summer occurred off campus. Chalmers' chief antagonist on the regents, Henry Bubb, head of Topeka's Capitol Federal Savings & Loan, pushed for the regents to fire him. KU, Bubb said, needed a "strong" administrator.

"He's a psychologist," Bubb said of the chancellor, "and he feels that if you leave things alone things will work themselves out. But you can't leave a powder keg alone with matches burning all around and not have something happen."

On July 26, a week and a half after the deaths of Rice and Dowdell, the regents met, voted on Bubb's motion and rejected it, 4-3. At the same meeting, the board voted to fire a black assistant to the dean of men who bought 27 boxes of ammunition in Topeka the day after Dowdell's shooting. The regents also formed a committee to study administrative hiring practices and

After two deaths and much turmoil in Lawrence, The Kansan *in July 1970 asked, "What happened?" Some answers, such as the full story behind two fatalities, would never be known.*

the allocation of student activity fees to campus groups.

Despite losing his motion to fire Chalmers, Bubb said, "I think it's obvious the chancellor's time is limited unless things change radically."

For his part, Chalmers went on a speaking tour of Kansas to explain the situation.

In the Kansas elections in August and November, politicians running on conservative platforms prospered. One was State Senator Reynolds Shultz of Lawrence, long a critic of the KU protesters and the administration, which in his view allowed protesters free rein. Shultz was elected lieutenant governor. Former Wichita Sheriff Vern Miller won the attorney general's office vowing to "land in Lawrence with both feet" to enforce state laws against drugs. Land he would in early 1971 with a series of drug raids in the city.

Meanwhile, the most radical of protest leaders stepped away or left town, according to Joel P. Rhodes in his *The Voice of Violence: Performative Violence as Protest in the Vietnam Era*. More moderate leaders took over the protest movement, but the movement itself divided along new lines.

Fall semester 1970 passed peacefully until early December. Then Gary Dean Jackson, the black assistant to the dean of men who was removed from his job by the regents for purchasing ammunition, went to the Board of Regents to appeal his case. In support of Jackson, members of the KU Black Student Union called for a student strike. They argued that Jackson should not have been fired without due process.

On the first morning of the strike, December 7, a white 22-year-old senior from Topeka confronted two black students who were painting the word "Strike" on the front of the Watson Library steps. He grappled with one of the two and was shot in the throat. The victim was hospitalized four days, but recovered.

The strike went on, but gained little campuswide support and after four days it was put on hold. Strike leaders said that fires and other incidents that had broken out during the strike were not the work of the BSU but were meant to implicate it.

A shooting and a bombing

With the strike called off and the end of semester approaching, the university on Friday, December 11, entered weekend mode. It would not remain that way.

Late that night, the telephone operator at the Computation Center in Summerfield Hall received a call saying a bomb would go off there in three minutes. Officials evacuated the building. The night outside was cold, however, and after a few minutes passed with no

A bowl, a Final Four and a world-class miler

In another of its periodic downturns, the KU football team won only two games in 1966 and the university fired nine-year Coach Jack Mitchell, replacing him with Pepper Rodgers. Deploying many of Mitchell's recruits, Rodgers engineered a surprising and brief upturn in the Jayhawks' fortunes.

His first season began with three straight losses, but then KU upset powerful Nebraska, 10-0. The team won four of its last six games, setting things up for an even better 1968.

With veteran players at most positions, the 1968 Jayhawks behind quarterback Bobby Douglass and defensive end John Zook reeled off seven straight victories before losing, 27-23, to a perennial Big Eight power, Oklahoma. KU closed with victories over Kansas State and Missouri, tied for the Big Eight championship and were invited to play in the Orange Bowl on New Year's night, 1969. The contest would serve as a landmark in football history, but at KU's expense.

Late in the game, the Jayhawks seemingly cemented a victory by turning back a Penn State attempt for a two-point conversion, stirring jubilation among the thousands of Kansas fans who had traveled to Miami. But the referees penalized KU for having too many players on the field. In what would become known as the "12th-man game," Penn State attempted another two-point conversion, this time against 11 KU players, and succeeded, taking a 15-14 lead with only seconds on the clock. Rarely had KU fans gone so rapidly from ecstasy to dejection.

The next year, KU descended to last place in the conference, winning only one of 10 games. By 1971 Rodgers had departed and Don Fambrough, a former player who had participated in the Orange Bowl after the 1947 season, took the reins. With David Jaynes as his sharp-throwing quarterback,

Closing with victories over Kansas State and Missouri, the Jayhawks would play in the Orange Bowl on New Year's night.

At the 1967 Kansas Relays, Jim Ryun finished the Glenn Cunningham mile run in 3:54.7.

Fambrough guided the Jayhawks through a nail-biting 1973 season of narrow conference victories and mostly narrow defeats plus a tie, ending at the Liberty Bowl in Memphis. KU lost that game, 31-18.

The basketball Jayhawks in 1971 reached the Final Four after losing only one regular-season game and ending with a perfect record in the Big Eight Conference. After defeating Houston and Drake in the Midwest Regional of the NCAA tournament in Wichita, the Jayhawks lost in the semifinal round at the Houston Astrodome to UCLA.

In the era, the football and basketball teams were led by excellent players, but another KU athlete became an international superstar, runner Jim Ryun from Wichita. In 1964, Ryun had become the first high-school runner to finish the mile in under four minutes. His high school coach, Bob Timmons, had committed to coach track at Oregon State in 1965 and Ryun planned to follow him there. But Timmons changed his mind after KU fired its coach and hired him, and so Ryan followed Timmons to Lawrence. He did not disappoint, running in the mile relay, the two-mile run and the 880-yard run. At the Kansas Relays in April 1966, Ryun set a meet record for the mile, and later that year at a meet in California set a world record, running the course in three minutes, 51 and three-tenths seconds. In early 1967, he followed with an even better time at another California meet, finishing in three minutes, 51 and one-tenth seconds. That record stood for eight years.

Hurdlers at the Kansas Relays, 1970.

explosion at least three of the evacuees decided to go back inside. Two of them were trying to open the doors and one was walking down a hall when a dynamite bomb exploded. It had been set amid boxes of computer paper and forms tucked under a stairwell. The stairwell and the reams of paper evidently cushioned some of the blast, and no one was seriously hurt.

The chancellor, who had been at a party when the explosion took place, came to the scene and called the culprit "pathological." Henry Bubb found it another instance of KU's allowing radical elements to act freely. Four days after the bombing, Bubb said at a regents meeting, "We've got to stop having so much permissiveness." Chalmers objected, but Bubb fired back, "If there's no permissiveness, it's odd that KU's the only campus where these things are happening."

As in the union fire, authorities never found who bombed the building. Chalmers survived the events of 1970, and violence subsided. Demonstrations continued, especially after the new attorney general, Vern Miller, led a well-publicized drug raid in late February 1971. A few days later, about 1,000 people gathered in front of Strong Hall to protest the raid as politically oriented.

In the 1971-72 academic year, things began to cool at KU, as they did at many American campuses. Protests occurred occasionally, but they were mostly peaceful and now arose from different causes.

In February 1972, 30 women's rights advocates, several KU faculty members, several students and four children, occupied an old house on the east edge of campus that was used by the East Asian Studies department. The occupiers called themselves the February Sisters. The group entered on the afternoon of February 4, a Friday, and after meeting from 2 a.m. until 7:30

Facing page: Students formed a crowded conga line in 1972.

a.m. with the chancellor and members of the Student Executive Committee, evacuated the building. They hoped by their action to persuade the university to open a daycare center, name a woman as vice chancellor for academic affairs, add a women to the staff to recruit women to KU, end hiring discrimination by sex, establish a department of women's studies and begin a women's health center.

Chalmers pointed to various actions already under way that answered some of their demands. The Student Executive Committee went to work on the child-care center, and eventually more of the demands were answered.

The Lawrence Gay Liberation Front, on the other hand, failed in its attempt at recognition by the university, leading to a lawsuit that a Topeka judge tossed out in February 1972.

The Vietnam war continued into 1972 and so did antiwar demonstrations. On May 10, 1972, demonstrators briefly occupied Chalmers' office, saying they wanted KU to investigate whether university research projects contributed to the U.S. role in Vietnam and to end any Endowment Association investments in war-related industries. The demonstrators left the chancellor's office, but remained in the hallways of Strong Hall for two nights.

The next day, protesters caused minor damage to the Military Science Building and Chalmers issued a warning that law enforcement would be called to halt more "disruptive acts." Nearly 30 people were arrested as crowds wandered the streets of Lawrence and the campus. Attorney General Miller showed up in front of the Kansas Union that same evening, warning people to clear the streets and ordering arrests. Chalmers criticized Miller for his action, and Miller replied, "I personally witnessed violations of the law, and when it became obvious that no attempts were being made to arrest, I ordered the arrests."

Protesters also staged a rally at the Kansas Relays.

The years had been as hard on the university as they had been trying for Chalmers. The Legislature kept KU on lean rations in fiscal 1971, when Governor Docking had used his line-item veto to restore some of the Legislature's cuts, and again in 1972. Under intense lobbying by administrators, alumni and student groups, the Legislature loosened the purse strings for fiscal 1973, granting an operating budget of $43.9 million. The amount represented a 5.73 percent increase over the year before. More than 1,000 faculty members got raises averaging more than 5 percent.

Meanwhile, a new school emerged in the era. Architecture and Urban Design was carved out of the School of Engineering. And more construction began on campus. By the beginning of fall semester 1971, chain link fences and covered wooden walkways lined the area across Jayhawk Boulevard from Strong Hall, where old Robinson Gymnasium and Haworth Hall had been removed. It marked the beginning of work on a new $7.8 million humanities building to be named Wescoe Hall in honor of the former chancellor. The structure was much reduced from the 25-story hilltop skyscraper envisioned by planners four years before, but large nevertheless. It would contain two auditoriums, scores of classrooms and hundreds of offices on its four levels. Workers also began building a new, $3 million student hospital along with a new building west of Iowa Street to house the Kansas Geological Survey.

A sudden end

In mid-August 1972, as the university prepared to open for fall semester, Chalmers' wife of 22 years sought and received an emergency divorce. Eight days later, the chancellor, blaming the stress of the divorce, submitted his resignation to the Board of Regents. He promised to vacate the chancellor's residence as quickly as he could.

Eight years afterward, Regent Henry Bubb said in an oral history donated to KU that the resignation took place after the chancellor's wife gave the regents a letter showing he was having an affair with another woman. Chalmers at first had denied the affair.

Chalmers' time as chancellor had lasted three tumultuous years and certainly his critics in Kansas were pleased at his departure. Yet Chalmers had his supporters, too. An editorial in *The Kansas City Times* pronounced Chalmers' departure "regrettable."

"If there are those who are not sorry to see Chalmers leave Lawrence, they are the same ones who would have answered campus problems with skull-cracking and massive expelling a couple of years ago," the editorial said. "Then there was talk of the chancellor's permissiveness."

What happened instead, the newspaper continued, was that KU emerged with relatively little damage "and its reputation intact." The wisdom of Chalmers' decisions, it said, "had become obvious."

Chalmers would go on to lead the Chicago Art Institute. In his place as chancellor, the regents named Raymond Nichols, a KU graduate and longtime executive secretary of the university.

Archie Dykes

Nichols had served five chancellors for more than 40 years and so had an intimate knowledge of the university's machinery. Although he held the office only until a new chancellor could be named, the regents removed "acting" from Nichols' title before he stepped down in mid-1973.

By then, the regents had chosen a permanent chancellor, 42-year-old Archie R. Dykes, head of the University of Tennessee at Martin. Dykes began work July 1. By then, KU

In February 1973, temperatures chilled. By then, campus protests had begun to do the same.

and other American campuses were cooling down, but their growth was heating up.

Projects that began in Chalmers' chancellorship reached completion early in Dykes' tenure. Wescoe Hall opened for classes in fall 1973. Earlier that year, the new home of the Kansas Geological Survey on west campus, Moore Hall, began operations. The new Watkins Memorial Health Center opened in 1974 and the old hospital next to Watson Library was converted into Twente Hall for the School of Social Welfare. Esther Twente had long been a member of the school faculty.

In 1971, the regents authorized a Wichita branch of the Medical Center, and the first class was admitted in 1974. In Kansas City, Kansas, in 1974 the School of Medicine was reorganized,

the nursing program was raised to full status as a school and a School of Allied Health was established.

In 1978 KU opened to the public the $3.5 million Spencer Museum of Art west of the Kansas Union. It was built through a gift from the Kenneth and Helen Spencer Foundation, then the largest single donation in KU history. Also added to campus were a new Green Hall for the School of Law and a new structure for the art and design program. In 1979, student fees helped build a Satellite Student Union near Allen Fieldhouse; within four years the union would be named after longtime Kansas Union Director Frank Burge.

In the early 1970s, the university studied demographic trends and forecast a substantial decline in enrollment in the 1980s. Nothing of the sort happened. Enrollments rose each year through the 1970s and reached 26,475 in 1980. Instead of dropping, they would stay steady through the first half of the decade and then rise most years afterward.

And the money rolled in. In Dykes' seven years as chancellor, KU's operating budget jumped from $98 million to $250 million. Even adjusting for the high inflation of the 1970s, that amounted to an increase of more than one-third.

Not all happy days

Along with all the new buildings, big donations and state largesse in the 1970s came more controversy and more headlines. They centered not on student protest but on faculty actions.

The Pearson Integrated Humanities Program lit one fire. Begun in 1971 by three professors, the program offered four semesters studying the great books of Western Civilization, all for college credit. Students also read Latin, traveled overseas, memorized poetry and studied the stars. The goal, according to its proponents, was to cut through rules surrounding coursework and give students a "real intellectual experience." Students entering the program could substitute Integrated Humanities courses for the regular English, speech, Western Civilization and humanities courses required of freshmen and sophomores in the College of Liberal Arts and Sciences.

As it developed, the program ran into opposition from faculty and others who contended it was taught dogmatically — from a single viewpoint — and shut out faculty who did not share the views of its three founders. Several of the great books studied contained the work of early Christian thinkers such as Thomas Aquinas, and parents of former students complained that the professors pushed Roman Catholicism in the classes. Indeed, several of its participants converted to Catholicism after joining the program, and some became monks.

Before the 1970s ended, the Integrated Humanities program was brought under the control of a special committee, its office in Wescoe Hall was closed and the program effectively ended.

In December 1979 and February 1980, a KU professor and former instructor visited Iran while 52 American hostages were being held there. The journeys of Professor Norman Forer and instructor Clarence Dillingham led to a brief controversy over faculty rights. For their time away from class, KU docked their pay, which led them to sue both Dykes and his successor. The suit later was dismissed.

Dykes also faced complaints about freedom of speech, one group demonstrating at commencement ceremonies over the matter.

"There are always issues," he told an interviewer in 1980. "It is the nature of the university to be a center of conflicting ideas with strong opinions on both sides of any issue."

In June that year, Dykes announced that he would leave to become head of Security Benefit Life Insurance Company of Topeka. Saying he wanted to move to the private sector, Dykes also mentioned how the chancellorship placed a draining demand on time.

"That's hard," he mused, "when you spend 12 to 14 hours a day at your job and still find someone who is unhappy with your performance."

Echoing a complaint made against his predecessor, Chalmers — that turmoil hadn't occurred nearly as much at other campuses as at KU — Dykes had this to say:

"Wherever you have alert, bright people, you're going to have controversy. It would bother me not to have discussion and controversy. It is a mark of greatness."

Facing page: Graduates marched down the hill,1972.

The Winning Game

On the night of May 12, 1988, 900 patrons of the University of Kansas filed into Crafton-Preyer Theatre at Murphy Hall. Wealthy former students and other friends of KU waited to hear about the beginning of the biggest private fund drive in school history.

The chancellor strode to the stage, escorted by a taller and even more widely known man named Danny Manning. Twenty-eight days earlier, Manning had led the basketball Jayhawks to the NCAA national championship in Kansas City.

On this night, the chancellor, Gene Budig, turned to shake Manning's hand. Instead, Manning offered him a high-five.

"This," Budig said, pointing to Manning, "is America's finest."

The chancellor followed sports keenly, just as he followed the realities of higher education. Manning and his teammates, Budig recognized, had accomplished more for KU than simply winning an important game. Jubilation could prove contagious. It could win friends for the university and it could open pocketbooks.

Rough going

The decade of the 1980s began unpleasantly for KU. The university found itself sailing into economic headwinds created by 10 percent

Gene Budig

inflation and tight state funding. At one point, Budig ordered air conditioning shut off on campus. He was well aware of how hot summers on the Great Plains could be.

A native of Nebraska, Budig had graduated from the University of Nebraska, worked as a reporter for newspapers in Lincoln and moved into academe, becoming an assistant to the Nebraska chancellor.

He went on to become president of Illinois State University and then of West Virginia University.

Budig was 41 when the Kansas Board of Regents picked him to be chancellor in March 1981. He arrived in June and embarked on a 60-county speaking tour of Kansas, trying to build support around the state for budget increases from the Legislature for salary and operating expenses.

In less than a year on the job, he found utility costs had outstripped the Legislature's appropriation, and ordered the sharp reduction in air conditioning. In Strong Hall, Budig held conferences inside in 90-degree temperatures. Across campus, administrators and faculty were advised to dress appropriately for the heat, keep hydrated and hold out until July 1, when more money would become available. That was only part of the effort. In 1982, Budig instituted cutbacks at the Medical Center, where a decline in patients at the hospital was generating less revenue. He ordered staff layoffs, hiring freezes and halts in purchases of some supplies.

Optimistic about the season to come, fans cheered coach Bill Self at 2009's "Late Night in the Phog."

Despite those efforts and others, the state still found revenues falling far short of projections. More cutbacks were necessary, so the regents instituted 4 percent spending cuts at their seven institutions. KU's share was more than $3 million. Immediately, the university halted hiring for vacant faculty and staff positions, and reduced money for travel and major expenses. The next year again was tough. The university cut $3.2 million more, and the chancellor said that academics were being affected.

All the university could do was try to dig its way out.

One method was to negotiate. In May 1983, the university, beset by high natural-gas bills, announced it would switch to oil as a fuel. Before the change was made, the gas company backed down and lowered rates.

Another way was to proselytize. Budig implored students and alumni, along with faculty and staff, to make KU's case to the state and thus to the Legislature. In summer 1986, Budig, interested in showing how KU benefited Kansas, announced he was forming a task force to study the university's role in the state economy. The state, he said, was "fighting for its economic life. Without KU's assistance, there is no possibility of significant economic development in the state."

Through those troubles, enrollment growth rarely faltered, and when it fell the drop was only a couple hundred. In August 1986 fall semester brought a record in Lawrence and at the Medical Center, with 28, 259 enrolled on both campuses. That created a housing crunch in Lawrence, and more than 225 students had to live in temporary space. Classrooms, too, felt the pressure.

"We have some classes where people don't even fit into the room," said Andrew Debicki, acting chairman of the department of Spanish and Portuguese.

Some faculty threw up their hands at the classroom sizes and at small pay increases and in February 1987 began to consider forming a union. In April, the regents approved a three-year plan to boost faculty salaries called "Margin of Excellence." Yet in August two organizations — the Kansas National Education Association and the American Association of University Professors — announced they would try to organize KU faculty in a collective-bargaining agreement. In November, faculty could vote on the matter. When the vote came, 440 or 52 percent of the voting faculty chose not to join either group, 216 voting for the KNEA and 191 for the AAUP. Of 1,017 eligible faculty, 847 cast ballots and the "No's" had it.

The turnaround

The basketball team in 1988, on which Manning was a senior, did not enter the NCAA tournament as world-beaters. The Jayhawks ended the regular season with 20 wins and 10 losses, finishing in third place in the Big Eight Conference. They lost in the finals of the Big Eight Tournament, but followed a charmed path through the opening rounds of the NCAA tournament, beating Xavier and Murray State in Lincoln, Nebraska, and Vanderbilt and Kansas State in Pontiac, Michigan.

The Final Four returned to Kansas City for its 50th anniversary, and KU began by upsetting Duke, 66-59, in the semifinal game in Kemper Arena. One month earlier, the Jayhawks had lost to the same team in Lawrence. In the championship game on April 4, KU and Oklahoma, which had beaten the Jayhawks twice in the regular season, raced to a 50-50 tie at halftime. KU pulled ahead in the second half, winning 83-79.

The team's success was the work not only of Manning but also of Coach Larry Brown, who had replaced Ted Owens for the 1983-1984 season. Brown had coached successfully in the NBA and in the college ranks at UCLA. In five years at KU, he had taken the Jayhawks to the NCAA tournament five times with one earlier trip

Trophy time, 1988: Jayhawk players held high the trophy for winning the NCAA national championship in basketball. After the game at Kemper Arena in Kansas City, the team returned to Lawrence for a confetti-strewn parade. Danny Manning, the team's dominant player, rode in this convertible.

to the Final Four.

By the late 1980s, the KU basketball team was the face of the university that the public could appreciate most often. In that decade, exposure of all sports was widened by the expansion of cable television with its scores of channels and all-sports networks. In 1988, the NCAA Tournament and the Final Four had already established themselves as a national celebration of basketball — and an important publicity boost for the university whose team won it all.

Small wonder that the fundraising drive that began a month later, called Campaign Kansas with a goal of raising $150 million in five years, featured Danny Manning at its opening. Yet his team's victory was not the only cause of exulting.

Budig also announced that a foundation started by former student and later real estate developer Ernst Lied had given $10 million for a new performing arts center. At the time, it was the largest gift in KU history.

Already, the university had pronounced 1988 its best budget year in a decade. The Legislature voted $9.15 million to improve faculty salaries, the first step in the Margin of Excellence program, and to boost other budgets.

Also in the works that year were a $13.9 million science library and a $12 million human development center to be named for Senator Robert Dole, who was instrumental in helping get federal money for the project. Planning got under way for a $5 million building for a KU Regents Center in south Overland Park to replace the one that had operated since 1975 at a former elementary school at 99th Street and Mission Road. Programs moved to the new Regents campus at 126th Street and Quivira Road in 1993. In Lawrence, Watson Library, Snow Hall and the Union received millions of dollars in renovations.

By September 1989, Campaign Kansas had

Facing page: Graduates strolled to the stadium amid a sea of well-wishers at commencement in May 2004.

gone so well that the goal was increased from $150 million to $177 million.

"KU has unprecedented momentum," Budig said.

Beyond the goal

Momentum in fundraising continued into the 1990s. Campaign Kansas exceeded even its reset goal and kept churning along until 1992, when it finally reached $262.9 million. From the drive had come money for professorships, scholarships, fellowships, student loans, libraries and academic programs.

Of all the gifts to the campaign, the Lied Foundation's remained the largest. Construction of the Lied Center on West Campus, west of Iowa Street, began in January 1991. By then the cost had risen to $14.3 million. At the same time, work was under way on a $14.8 million biomedical research building for the Medical Center.

The KU endowment ranked ninth largest among public universities in the United States. In 1991, fall enrollment on all campuses surpassed 29,000.

But not all was roses. On June 15, 1991, a lightning strike set fire to Hoch Auditorium, gutting it and causing $12.8 million in damage. The building had no lightning rods.

At least one thing was different from the 1960s, when Fraser met its end with last-minute and disorganized opposition. Members of the Historic Mount Oread Fund, a unit of the Endowment Association, organized a campaign stressing to KU officials their hope that at least the façade of Hoch could be saved. The state, after first balking, freed up money from a federal payment in 1992, and the Legislature allotted more money to plan and rebuild the structure. The final bill totaled $23 million. The façade stood, so the streetscape along that section of Jayhawk Boulevard retained its appearance

The regents named the new structure Budig Hall. In a bow to tradition, "Hoch Auditoria" was

1982's best homecoming float with non-moving parts, won by Alpha Omicron Pi and Pi Kappa Alpha.

placed on a sign in front. The building, containing a 1,000-seat auditorium and two 500-seat lecture halls equipped with multimedia teaching technology, was rededicated in 1997.

By then, Gene Budig was no longer chancellor. A confirmed baseball fan, Budig in summer 1994 accepted a dream job — president of the American League. The position, he said, offered new challenges and new scenery.

In Budig's 13-year tenure, he had overseen an ambitious building program and steady increases in enrollment, and added more than 180 faculty. He worked ably with legislators and regents in support of the university. His crowning achievement perhaps was the fundraising effort that he had kicked off with Danny Manning at his side, Campaign Kansas.

Eve of a new century

Throughout KU history, each chancellor set lofty goals for educational excellence. Excellence required salaries big enough to attract capable faculty, and funds to build classrooms and laboratories and to pay for equipment and research. Over many of KU's 150 years, legislators and governors fell short of providing enough state money to accomplish all that.

Making up the difference required long hours of tapping donors. It also called for well-oiled publicity machinery to keep tens of thousands of alumni knowledgeable and supportive. In a tight financial environment, it also required charging students and their parents more to be a Jayhawk, through higher tuitions.

Less than six months after Budig's departure, the regents in early January 1995 placed the tasks of chancellor in the hands of Robert Hemenway. Since 1989, Hemenway had been chancellor of the main campus at the University of Kentucky, where he had also served on the English faculty and been chairman of the English Department. The 53-year-old Hemenway, like Budig a native of Nebraska, earned his bachelor's at Nebraska-Omaha and his doctorate at Kent State. He had also taught at the University of Wyoming and been dean of arts and sciences at the University of Oklahoma.

He began work at KU officially on June 1, 1995.

As the son of two educators, Hemenway said, he inherited a passion for reading, writing

KU's Edwards Campus in Overland Park.

and teaching. His father's own storytelling skills, he said, encouraged him to value that art and to practice it himself. In his college studies Hemenway immersed himself in English literature, and he found himself valuing the storytelling techniques of Richard Wright, Ralph Ellison and other black authors. Hemenway wrote the definitive biography of Zora Neale Hurston, a nearly forgotten black novelist, folklorist and anthropologist of the 1930s. *The New York Times* listed the book as among the best of 1978.

More so than his predecessor, Hemenway made it a practice to be visible on campus, a trait that followed him from his days at Kentucky. Sack lunch in hand, he liked to sit with groups of students at mid-day to talk. The regents who chose him valued, among other things, his sense of humor, which he and they hoped would defuse the testy situations in which chancellors found themselves.

In the years to come, Hemenway would use amiability, humor and storytelling smarts to guide the university through rough waters.

Trials of a new administration

On taking office in summer 1995, the new chancellor inherited a $3 million reduction in the budget — the result partly of a Legislature that had begun to question closely all spending on higher education and partly of a shortfall in expected federal research money. Already, the university had delayed faculty and staff raises for six months, so as he entered office Hemenway faced a restive group of employees. To overcome the rest of the shortage the administration recommended cuts in academic programs, in research and in graduate studies, along with holding vacant 10 faculty and 54 other full-time jobs.

In addition, only a couple of months before Hemenway's arrival it came to light that the heart-transplant program at the KU Medical Center had performed no transplants for 10 months. It had

Hoch Auditorium was gutted by fire in 1991. Its replacement, Budig Hall, below, preserved Hoch's collegiate gothic look outside, and inside featured the latest technology.

rejected all donor hearts during that same period, and told none of the 14 patients on the waiting list for a heart. In fact, it added patients during that period. Meanwhile, it billed those waiting patients half a million for heart-related services, including $420,000 for hospital charges.

Robert Hemenway

The program was shut down in April 1995. The attorney general fined the Medical Center and two of its foundations $265,000 and much of that was distributed among patients and their families.

Even before the heart-transplant problem was revealed in *The Kansas City Star*, the Medical Center had come under fire from legislators for administrative difficulties and sloppy housekeeping. On June 7, 1995, in Hemenway's first week on the job, he appointed a new executive vice chancellor for the Medical Center, the retiring Navy surgeon general, Donald Hagen.

The cost of education

As for budget shortfalls, part of the response by the regents and the university was to raise tuitions. It became a difficult but common practice through the next few years.

In 1997, for any legislator or Kansan willing to listen, KU made its point: Over the preceding two decades, the share of the state general fund budget for regents institutions had dropped from 20 percent to 13.6 percent. In that same period, tuitions as a percentage of overall educational costs had risen from 21.9 percent to 43 percent.

At KU and Kansas State University, the regents calculated, in-state tuition had grown 285.5 percent. By comparison in those same 20 years, the Consumer Price Index had risen 161.3 percent. But tuition would continue to carry an increasing part of the load at state institutions.

The tuition increases directly affected KU's campus demographics. The number of out-of-state students, who paid higher fees than Kansans, began to diminish. From 1995 to 1996 alone, non-resident enrollment fell by 400 but resident enrollment by only 25.

In fact, total enrollment had dropped since the early 1990s, when it peaked above 29,000. By 1996, the fall semester total was counted at 27,407. Dormitory rooms stood empty and Hemenway encouraged more efforts to recruit students.

Any greater efforts, however, would run headlong into a more tuition increases. In 2002, the Legislature responded to a reduction in state revenue by slashing $7.1 million from the previous year's total for aid to KU. The university announced that, for the first time in 30 years, it would not give regular raises. By December of that year, it had laid off 44 people, lowered thermostats, cut library hours and asked faculty members to do their own clerical tasks.

In addition, KU sought and the regents approved a 25 percent tuition increase, the largest since 1970. That alone generated $14 million, offsetting the state cuts. In 2003 came another tuition increase, this one nearly 21 percent. In 2004, the bump was 18 percent.

Finally, in 2007, to ease the planning burden on students and their families, KU implemented a program enabling incoming freshmen to pay the same fixed rate for the four years of their education. Full-time Kansas students entering school that fall would pay $3,408 a semester and out-of-state students $8,960.

In 2008 total fall enrollment reached 30,000. The university, officials said, had run out of classroom and laboratory space and once again dormitories had filled up.

Searching for ways to increase revenue, Hemenway proposed to spin off the hospital from the Medical Center, removing it from most state controls in hopes it would generate more money. Because of the way budgets were set by the Legislature, changes in hospital spending plans often required up to two years to make. In the quickly morphing climate of health insurance, and particularly the growth of managed-care plans, that was too much time to take advantage of changes. The hospital operation lost potential revenue to its competitors in the Kansas City metropolitan area.

After much negotiating and campaigning by Hemenway and others, the Legislature in 1998 approved the idea of a separation. A difficult agreement was hammered out among the hospital, the Medical Center and KU Physicians Inc. In the end, the KU Hospital struck out on its own and the plan worked.

From the beginning of his chancellorship, Hemenway had sought to increase spending on research, particularly in bioscience. At the end of his first five years, he pointed to an increase from $90 million to $193 million. By 2008, it rose to nearly $300 million. That year KU got $20.2 million from the National Institutes of Health, the largest federal research award in Kansas history. Meanwhile, more than $150 million had gone into construction of new research laboratories.

Not missing a beat — or bounce

Bolstered by money from television, ticket sales and sports-loving contributors, college athletics by the 1990s served as a primary engine of public relations and alumni loyalty and pride.

Right after winning the 1988 NCAA championship, the basketball team lost both its star, Danny Manning, and its coach, Larry Brown, to the professional ranks. Athletic Director Bob Frederick replaced Brown with a little-known assistant from North Carolina, Roy Williams.

In his first season, with his team on probation and banned from postseason play for earlier transgressions, Williams' Jayhawks won 19 games and lost 12. The next year, Williams

Wearing a straw hat to fend off the hot sun, Chancellor Hemenway spoke at commencement in 2001.

took the Jayhawks to the NCAA tournament, beginning a string of appearances that continued well into the 21st century. KU reached the Final Four in 1991 and 1993, 2002 and 2003, and won or tied for the conference championship nine times.

For football, after several dreary seasons the 1990s began in similar fashion. In 1992 the Jayhawks won their first bowl game in 31 years, the Aloha Bowl in Hawaii, and returned to the islands in 1995, winning the Aloha Bowl again. Just before that game, Coach Glen Mason announced he was leaving to coach at Georgia, and then changed his mind. He stayed only one more year before departing for the University of Minnesota. Not until 2005 would the Jayhawks have another winning football season.

In 2001, even the Athletic Department faced financial cutbacks. With a projected debt of $650,000 on the horizon in the year to come, Athletic Director Bob Fredrick ended KU men's swimming and tennis. He was flooded with angry calls and emails, and about 75 people gathered in front of the chancellor's residence to protest. At the end of April, Frederick resigned.

KU commissioned a search firm to find candidates to replace Frederick and it came up with four, who were interviewed by a committee named by the chancellor. Their choice was the athletic director at Fresno State, Al Bohl.

He did not go over well.

Bohl's style was much like that of an energetic pitch man; some called it "rah-rah." He proved to be an ineffective leader and wound up annoying segments of the Athletic Department, alumni, donors and coaches. Few were more important to KU's well-being than Roy Williams, who was rumored to be have been dissatisfied about Bohl's firing football coach Terry Allen with three games to go in a season.

April 2003 Al Bohl was fired just as the basketball team lost the national championship game to Syracuse. Despite Bohl's departure Williams himself departed within days of the final game to coach at his alma mater, North Carolina.

To pick a new athletic director, Hemenway this time rejected using a search firm or a large committee. He worked with Drew Jennings, the interim athletic director, and came up with Lew Perkins of the University of Connecticut.

Before Perkins was hired, Jennings found a replacement for Williams as coach: Bill Self from the University of Illinois. Self picked up where his predecessor left off, winning a string of conference championships, reaching the NCAA

The KU Hospital in Kansas City, Kansas. Below: the JayDoc mascot joined a semester-ending get-together in 2003 with a graduate, left, and her daughter.

Coaching generations, then to now

KU's string of successful basketball teams and coaches began after the game's inventor, James Naismith, started the program and compiled a losing record overall. W.O. Hamilton's 10 teams won twice as many games as they lost. Then came Phog Allen.

KU's living coaches gathered in October 2014. Below, as they appeared coaching...

Bill Self   Larry Brown   Roy Williams   Ted Owens   Dick Harp

In 1997, the university dedicated a statue of Allen outside the field house named for him. Chancellor Hemenway looked up with Robert Allen, the coach's son. Allen was followed by Dick Harp. Allen died in 1974, Harp in 2000.

tournament each year and delivering a national championship in 2008.

Perkins, meanwhile, boosted revenues; one method was to allocate prime seats for basketball based on the size of the ticket buyer's donation to KU athletics. His work succeeded, and in February 2006, KU announced plans to build a new $31 million football facility at Memorial Stadium. Football coach Mark Mangino, hired by Bohl, hailed it as an important boost for his improving program.

By the end of the new century's first decade, Perkins would depart in the wake of a federal investigation into a ticket scam operated by several employees of the athletic department. He would be replaced by Sheahon Zenger. Football

coaches would come and go, as they had for decades.

Basketball, which since the 1920s provided KU's highest and most consistent attainments in the major sports, remained one of the university's chief ambassadors to its alumni — where the need for friends grew larger with the passing years.

Sheahon Zenger

The search for money

At the dawn of the new century in 2001, KU launched its third capital campaign, which set a goal of $500 million. Called KU First: Invest in Excellence, the fundraising effort had

KU won the 2008 NCAA national championship, beating the University of Memphis in San Antonio.

quietly gathered $280 million by the time of the announcement.

That number contained the largest gift in university history, $42 million from the Hall Family Foundation, which represented the owners of Hallmark Cards of Kansas City. The funds, to be given over five years beginning in 2001, would go to life sciences research at the Medical Center, expansion of the KU campus in Overland Park, endowed chairs in the humanities, the School of Business and remodeling of the Hall Center for the Humanities next to Watson Library in Lawrence.

The KU Endowment Association in mid-2001 reported assets of $1.06 billion. In the preceding year, that money had generated $62 million for KU, or about 8 percent of its total revenue. Contributions, indeed, formed an important component of the university's economic life.

In 2003, the campaign met its $500 million goal and raised the bar to $600 million. Donors crossed that line and went beyond. In June 2005, KU First came to an end, having gathered $653 million.

Research efforts got $132 million, and $97 million would go to buildings. Faculty received $65.5 million and the number of endowed professorships rose from 100 to 165.

For students, there was more than $100 million, most of it in scholarships. The handsome gifts, Hemenway said, enabled KU to recruit "the very best and brightest students" in the Midwest.

A leadership change

In December 2008, Hemenway, now 67 years old, said he would retire as chancellor on June 30, 2009. He had overcome annual budget hurdles, raised millions of dollars, overseen hundreds of millions in construction, and watched as enrollment topped 30,000. Eleven months before his announcement, the Jayhawk football team under Coach Mark Mangino and quarterback Todd Reesing won the Orange Bowl, 24-21, over Virginia Tech. In April the Jayhawk basketball team under Self won the NCAA national championship.

Hemenway's tenure lasted 14 years, the third longest in university history after Ernest Lindley's and Frank Strong's. His top stated goal had been to raise KU's status as a research university and he had garnered many millions in that cause. Hemenway's name would go on the new Life Sciences Innovation Center at the Medical Center.

His successor broke new ground in the roll of chancellors, all of whom had had been white men. She was Bernadette Gray-Little, the first African-American and the first woman to lead the university.

The Board of Regents announced the selection on May 29, 2009, and a little more than a month later she officially succeeded to the chancellor's office. The 64-year-old Gray-Little, a native of North Carolina, had been an administrator and member of the psychology faculty at the University of North Carolina.

"I hope this is a great day for KU," she said. "It is a wonderful day for me."

Like all her predecessors as chancellor, she would face the need to raise money to offset a decline in state funding.

Gray-Little took office near the depth of a nationwide recession, and in the middle of her first year Governor Mark Parkinson announced

Bernadette Gray-Little

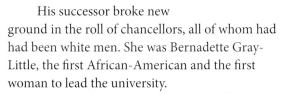

Fundriaising campaign logo

that big new cuts would have to be made in light of falling revenues. Public universities and colleges, he said, would lose $2 million on top of $100 million in earlier reductions. Those had caused the regents once again to raise tuition. State support for higher education now descended to what it had been in 2006.

In April 2012 the university launched another fundraising campaign called "Far Above." The name came from the first two words of the alma mater. The goal was the biggest of any campaign to date, $1.2 billion. Because fundraising had gotten underway quietly beforehand, by May 2012 the drive had raised $612 million.

In addition, KU aimed to increase money for research and to improve the university's graduation rate. Two years later, the university unveiled a five-year strategic plan it named Bold Aspirations, part of which entailed finding ways to reach those goals. In its first three years it tested new ways to present courses, particularly to large groups of students. Also it moved to improve recruitment, retention and funding for doctoral students. For faculty, post-tenure review was updated. Efficiencies to save money were part of the plan, too; shared service centers consolidated some financing and budgeting operations.

As the United States emerged from the worst of the recession, the university and other institutions of higher education climbed out of the budget mess, with lots of help from donors. In April 2010, ground was broken for a third building at KU's campus in Overland Park, which had been named for longtime supporters Roy and Joan Edwards. Thirteen years earlier, the site had only one structure.

In October 2012 KU sought to restore faculty to the size it had been before hiring slowed in the early 2000s. The university announced it would seek 64 new faculty in engineering and other disciplines. The same month, the Capitol Federal Foundation gave $20 million for a new building for the School of Business. In May 2014, the Hall Family Foundation gave money for construction of a $75 million education building at the Medical Center.

A decade-long push to bring the KU Cancer Center designation as an official partner of the National Cancer Institute culminated in success in summer 2012. The move opened the door to millions of dollars in federal grants and more private funds toward preventing, diagnosing and treating cancer. KU had raised and invested about $350 million in the project.

The state, however, continued to limit its contribution. Budget cuts authorized by the 2013 Legislature were projected to cost KU $13.5 million over the next two years.

The proud record of the years

One hundred fifty years ago, there was little doubt that Kansas would have a university. What no one knew was how big and how good it would turn out to be. In 1866, in its first fall semester, the University of Kansas counted only 55 students, none of whom did work at college level. Today, it has more than 27,000 students, and they are pursuing baccalaureate degrees, master's degrees and doctorates of philosophy, not to mention degrees in law, medicine and other professions. More than a quarter list themselves as being part of a minority.

In the 1860s, the faculty began with only three members and in years to come did not back down from confrontation with administrators. In 2014, faculty on the Lawrence campus totaled more than 1,600 with 1,000-plus more at the Medical Center. In the spirit of their predecessors, many remain outspoken.

The state that created the university still wavers in its support, just as it has for a century and a half. In the 10 years ending in 2013, state money fell from more than 27 percent of KU's revenue to about 20 percent. As a result, the university has turned to students and their families to pay increasing amounts of tuition and fees. Their percentage of KU revenue increased from less than 15 percent in 2003 to 22 percent in 2013. Grants and research contracts generate an even larger share of revenue.

As it has throughout its history KU also relies on gifts from generous alumni and friends — about $1 in every $10 in revenue — to maintain its quest for excellence. The Endowment Association's motto remains accurate: "To build a greater university than the state alone can build."

In Lawrence alone, the campus sprawls across about a thousand acres, a far cry from the original three-story building and its tiny acreage on the crest of the hill. A glance at the official campus map today puts the geographical center somewhere near Allen Fieldhouse. From KU's inception, that center has shifted west and south from the first building on the northern tip of Mount Oread. And that's not counting the Medical Center in Kansas City, Kansas, or the Edwards Campus in Overland Park.

As the campus grew, other buildings filled in the empty spots —but not all of them. Wisely, KU carved out greenswards and groves that made and kept it the beautiful place envisioned by James Marvin more than a century and a quarter ago.

The look of the place helps students fall in love with it and alumni stay in love, cemented by experiences: this inspirational professor and that life-changing class, winter nights in a packed fieldhouse and autumn afternoons at the stadium, favorite roommates and romances, and even long evenings of carousing.

In fact, the final proof that the dreams of 1866 were met and exceeded over the next century and a half is in the memories of all the people who have called themselves Jayhawks.

The way a Jayhawk looks, maybe

1912

1917

1970

For more than a century, artists and artisans have worked to personify the Jayhawk. The first generally accepted attempt was Henry Maloy's, above left. Mascot uniforms mimic illustrated versions, which appeared in various publications and forms through the years. None was commissioned by KU until Hal Sandy's version in 1946.

1966

1912

1920

1923

1929

1941

1946

The way a Jayhawk looks, really

At commencement in May 2014, Chancellor Gray-Little urged graduates to take and send in "selfies." Here are some of the faces in the last graduating class before KU's 150th anniversary year.

Sources

Any survey of the history of KU has to begin with the three existing volumes about its history. Clifford Griffin, a professor of history, wrote a well-researched account of the university's first century, *The University of Kansas: A History*. In it, Griffin described the intricate battle over the site of the planned state university, the nearly constant fuss over money with the state, the changing rules of university governance, the heroes of the faculty and the life of the students. That volume was published by the University Press of Kansas in 1974.

In the middle of the 20th century, a KU chemistry professor, Robert Taft, wrote a volume of remembrances about various events and people through the university's history. His first effort, published in 1941, was *Across the Years on Mount Oread, 1866-1941: An Informal and Pictorial History of the University*

of Kansas. In 1955, he added to that book in his *The Years on Mount Oread: A revision and extension of Across the Years on Mount Oread*. The book breaks its subject into individual accounts.

In the 1980s, three authors with close ties to the university compiled a pictorial history, *On the Hill: A Photographic History of the University of Kansas*. The compilers were Virginia Adams, Katie Armitage, Donna Butler, Carol Shankel and Barbara Watkins.

More recently, a website, **kuhistory. com**, has brought to the internet a wealth of information about individual people and events in the history of the University of Kansas. The articles are written by faculty in the Department of History, and by others in various departments of KU, and are thorough and well-crafted. The website stemmed from the KU History Project, which in its earliest

days was overseen by Henry Fortunato and produced scores of articles under the title, "This Week in KU History." Later, Mike Reid assumed leadership of the project.

Other sources of information for this survey included issues of *The Lawrence Journal World* and its predecessors in Lawrence journalism, *The Kansas City Star* and *The Kansas City Times* and *The Topeka Capital Journal* and its predecessors. The *Jayhawker* yearbook and its variously named predecessor yearbooks were valuable for their accounts of various years as well as for the images of life on campus.

No repository contains close to as many images about KU as the University Archives at the Kenneth Spencer Research Library, where Rebecca Schulte and her staff preserve and make available a wide array of items.

Photographs and illustrations

The majority of the images in this book came from the University Archives at the **Kenneth Spencer Research Library, University of Kansas Libraries**. Rebecca Schulte, the University Archivist, and others on the staff have a wide-ranging knowledge of the Archives' holdings, which are plentiful.

Because of the large number of those images, the University Archives credit will not be repeated here for each item. Instead, the reader should assume an image is from the **Kenneth Spencer Research Library, University of Kansas Libraries**, unless otherwise noted.

Index

I'm A Jay Hawk

Words and Music by
GEO. BOWLES, '08 - '11

Talk a-bout the soon-ers the Ag-gies and the braves,

Talk a-bout the tig-er and his tail,_____ Talk a-bout the husk-ers, those

old corn-hus-kin' boys, But I'm a bird to make 'em weep and wail._____